A System at Risk

A System at Risk

✦

The Economics of Transportation

Dr. Harold W. Worrall

iUniverse, Inc.
New York Lincoln Shanghai

A System at Risk
The Economics of Transportation

iUniverse books may be ordered through booksellers or by contacting:

iUniverse
2021 Pine Lake Road, Suite 100
Lincoln, NE 68512
www.iuniverse.com
1-800-Authors (1-800-288-4677)

ISBN-13: 978-0-595-36643-9 (pbk)
ISBN-13: 978-0-595-67398-8 (cloth)
ISBN-13: 978-0-595-81065-9 (ebk)
ISBN-10: 0-595-36643-0 (pbk)
ISBN-10: 0-595-67398-8 (cloth)
ISBN-10: 0-595-81065-9 (ebk)

Printed in the United States of America

Contents

List of Illustrations

List of Figures

List of Tables

Acknowledgements

With great pleasure, I would like to acknowledge those who have contributed and inspired me along the way. First, I acknowledge my wife Jean for her support when times were difficult and inspiration was a scarce commodity and for her help in proof reading. I would also like to thank my son Lonnie for helping design the book cover.

Dr. James Wright and Dr. Wendell Lawther reviewed the book in the early stages and offered guidance during the process and I am very grateful for their help and friendship. To Boglarka Szollosi for her assistance in providing research support for some of the more difficult topics, thank you. I wish to thank Dan Greenbaum of Vollmer Associates whose tremendous experience with traffic models provided valuable insight on the subject of congestion growth rates and to Dr. Essam Radwan for reviewing my work in this area.

Finally, I wish to thank my students who for each of the last ten years have taught me to see the world of transportation policy from a new and fresh perspective.

Preface

This work comes at a point in my career when one era of transportation is ending and the next is being formulated. I started my career in transportation in 1969 as a graduate engineer. I was starting in the latter stages of the construction of one of the greatest public works projects in history, the interstate highway system. As my transportation career morphed over the course of three plus decades, I was fortunate to participate in engineering, finance, information technology and toll operations for several state transportation agencies both as a consultant and as an employee. Along the way, I earned an MBA and finally a PhD in public policy. I have had the opportunity to travel to China, Australia and throughout the European Union and understand their programs for transportation and public/private delivery systems. I have come to understand that the economic context for deciding the transportation policy for the U.S. is global not national and the directions chosen must focus on the arterial highway system.

The interstate system fed an economic boom of enormous magnitude and recently it has begun to congest with the growing traffic resulting from truck freight and passenger movement. We have continued to use all the highways as if there is no limit to capacity and have slowly forgotten the connection between gasoline tax and the provision of capacity. Many now perceive the use of highways as a "free" public good. While there was sufficient capacity for the economic expansion, there was no direct impact on our daily lives, and transportation was an issue that ranked far behind many others such as crime, education and health care.

Suddenly, transportation has become an issue and a topic of great concern. We have begun to realize that there is a connection to continued economic growth and the ability to compete globally. However, the picture of what the issues are and what we should do next still seems a bit blurry. My hope is that this book will provide some clarity and contribute to the process of formulating a direction for our considerable energies. Though we realize that an issue exists, there is little appreciation for how we got here, how large the issue might be or how quickly we must respond.

Our economic success as a nation is inherently linked to the efficiency of our transportation system and they are in jeopardy. For an entire century, the United States has developed on the assumption of plentiful, cheap gasoline and a highway system that is perceived as a free commodity. We are dependent upon the automobile for passenger travel and increasingly the truck for freight transportation. Not only has that dependence continued it has grown to the point that highway congestion threatens drastic effects to the national economy. Our ability to change the behavior of the individual transportation customer is severely limited in a free democratic society and attempting to affect this dynamic through policy has had limited effect. We have encouraged and subsidized mass transit and all the while purchasing more Sport Utility Vehicles, SUV's and automobiles and driving all of them further. We have tried to encourage the efficient movement of freight while experiencing significant growth in highway freight transportation.

Much has been done in the last thirty years to provide alternative modes of transportation in the United States however, our transportation capacity remains inexorably tied to the rubber tire vehicle. The reasons are many but the fact is undeniable. Though we attempt to develop transportation policy to wean ourselves from the open highway, we return to it in automobiles and SUVs in increasing numbers. We do so out of a desire for convenience and the need to accommodate schedules that are ever more hectic. Concurrently, more freight is being delivered "just in time" by tractor-trailer combinations to assembly lines and retail operations. This increasing demand has continued unabated and concurrently little or no new highway capacity has been added.

Our surface transportation system is the evolution of a patchwork of transportation policy decisions over nearly two centuries of economic progress. It is the result of a swirling mix of changing politics, business lobbying, economic decision-making and evolution. The perception and expectation of the citizenry is that transportation, especially highways, should be "free" and that sufficient funds already exist to provide highways, if only the public sector were as efficient as business. We have been lulled into a sense of peace and continued prosperity arising out of the existence of superior highway systems typified by the interstate highway system. Though we have shown leadership and even daring in the past we have become increasingly unwilling as a society to address the issue economically or politically.

Through the prism of transportation economics, the case is presented that we are fast approaching a crisis, one that will directly affect our ability to compete in the global marketplace. The ability to move people and goods over great distances quickly, at low cost and in a flexible manner has produced tremendous economic growth in the United States. This transportation system is at risk from the effects of accelerating congestion.

Growing congestion also jeopardizes the safety of the traveling public. Such safety concerns entail great personal and economic costs that must be born by the public. With more vehicles competing for the same space, accidents become more likely, which create delay and the likelihood of further incidents. All of this significantly reduces highway capacity. Taken in combination, the effect is a drag on economic efficiency.

There is little doubt in the academic community that an inherent close relationship between transportation and economic vitality exists. It is fundamental that the movement of people and goods is inherent in a healthy economy. What is not well understood is the definition of this relationship in specificity. At the core of the transportation/economic relationship are the concepts of time utility and place utility, critical to understanding the economic link. Further proof of this relationship will be demonstrated by a review of the economics of competition and a brief review of history.

With the relationship established, the question of immediacy arises. How long will it take the transportation crisis to occur? What if nothing is changed? What are the risks if transportation policy and practice remain unaltered?

The impending crisis is only beginning to become evident, predominantly in urban areas. Congestion rate statistics reveal growing travel times that convert directly to economic inefficiency, reduced safety, damage to the environment and an overall lowering of the quality of life. Over the last forty years the United States population has grown, urbanized, suburbanized and has become more mobile. For a sometime, mobility was served by the construction of the interstate highway system and the accompanying urban arterial network.

Freight traffic has inherently grown with the economy. The demand for more flexibility in the delivery of goods and the introduction of "just-in-time" inventory control has resulted in rapid growth in rubber tire freight traffic. This heavy vehicle traffic growth combined with automobile traffic growth is a recipe for poor safety. Vehicles with vastly different acceleration/deceleration characteristics, residing on the same increasingly congested highway is a fertile environment for reduced safety and higher costs to society overall.

While these are momentous national issues for the United States, they should also be viewed in a global context. Global economic competition and the global exchange of goods and services is a reality. It is significant that nations, such as China, are showing strong sustained growth in economic power and other nations are confederating into larger and more efficient economic units, such as the European Union. These countries have recognized the need to improve transportation systems and they have defined the transportation investments necessary to support continued economic growth. To remain competitive, the United States must renew its vigor to have a well-planned, well-funded and aggressively implemented surface transportation system.

The subject of transportation policy in America is not simple but is understandable. We are the envy of the world in terms of our ability to move people and goods by public highway, air transportation, water transport and rail, whether public or private. We have been living off of one of the greatest public works projects in the history of mankind, (the interstate highway system) all the while obfuscating this fact with elaborate treatises promoting "silver bullets" and serving short term political agendas at the expense of our future. To analyze the issues of transportation we must first dissect the greater transportation question into its component subsystems.

It is not sufficient and many times not helpful to the public agenda to discuss transportation generically. Statements about what we should do to improve transportation too often overlook the various and variable facets of the issue. What may be true in the urban area is not true in the rural areas of America. What is true for freight movement might not hold for passenger traffic. What is true in one part of the country may not be true in another. A discussion of the issues of transportation in the United States are therefore segmented into urban-rural and freight-passenger, resulting in four basic categories for analysis. The prescription for improvement is based upon this multifaceted analysis.

For the United States to globally compete long term will require a change in our assumptions about transportation and our model of implementing transportation solutions. While much can be said for and against our methods of planning for transportation systems, it is in the implementation stage that our greatest challenges exist. We must begin to think like a business without the requirement to be one. We must seriously consider private sector models for financing, operating and managing some of our country's greatest assets. Government is capable of functioning under private sector models but the "public trust" must be held paramount. Concurrently, we must not assume that public agencies are required to provide public goods. Private sector ownership and capital investment can be complementary to the public process. Financing public transportation infrastructure in the future will require a balance of public and private resources.

Funding of public infrastructure in the United States has evolved within the doctrine of equity (fair share) to the detriment of efficiency. A balance must be struck between the two based on market forces rather than political forces. We must realize that current funding methods are inadequate and consider other scenarios based on pricing and demand management that create a potential for balancing equity and efficiency through market driven mechanisms. Finance plans must take into account the time value of money and the loss of buying power as projects are delayed. Further, we must begin to realize that opportunity costs resulting from delay are perhaps the largest economic loss.

Finally, the concept of a nexus or linkage between use and cost must exist. It should not be surprising that demand has outstripped the ability of public agencies to provide a public good whose perceived cost is zero. Attempting to fund public infrastructure on a "pay-as-you-go," categorical funding basis stimulates delay introduced by waiting for sufficient funds to be accumulated to construct. The many categories of funds also restrict flexibility of funding.

Why haven't we recognized the urgency and adopted some of these techniques? First and foremost is the lack of understanding of the critical nature of delaying needed transportation facilities. Second is the confusion resulting from an overly complex funding process devised more for encouraging policy adherence and ensuring equitable allocation by geographical region than efficiently funding needed transportation infrastructure. United States transportation policy must focus on maintaining current transportation advantages such as the Interstate system and leverage crucial transportation corridors. The networks of rail, highway, pipeline, waterways and air corridors are established and well traveled. Our strategic future use of these assets may well determine our global competitiveness.

Policy is inherently political and a great challenge is political courage. It is extremely difficult for political leaders to take long-term views when reelection cycles are short term and "silver bullets" rarely fail in the timeframe of an election cycle. Political courage can result in the loss of an election. It is often more expedient to satisfy a vocal minority expounding a popular myth especially one that enjoys the support of sensational press coverage. It may be more politically convenient to support minor reallocations of funds which satisfy influential special interest groups or constituencies than to attempt major transportation policy alteration. These failures of political courage incrementally accumulate and culminate in a threat to economic vitality.

The question of economic competitiveness and the necessity to take bold action in transportation finance, project delivery and taxation policy center on the concept of pricing transportation. Direct user fees will re-establish the price and use relationship, generate much of the necessary funding and do so in a way that affects the demand for transportation.

This book is about economic competition, the intimate role of transportation in that competition and the prescriptions necessary to create a self-sustaining system of transportation funding and the major changes needed in the delivery systems to provide transportation in an efficient manner. When these funding and delivery systems are brought together, price will be reintroduced into the decision making of the traveling public and more funding will be available to provide transportation to all levels of society. It is intended to draw the attention of the citizenry and the transportation policy makers alike to the probability that the future for transportation in America and the accompanying economic success of America is in jeopardy. Our economic malaise is not the result of the internet bubble, corporate greed or other short term factors alone, it results from a long term transportation generated, economic pathology only now beginning to be felt. It is my hope that this book will bring new focus to the debate on United States transportation policy.

This work does not address questions of social justice and ensuring equal access to transportation. Access to an automobile in America has become synonymous with transportation access. Without an automobile in many parts of the United States, individuals are disenfranchised from employment, recreation, education and the basic freedoms that comprise quality of life. While a critical consideration to the construct of a true Republic and inherently relevant to transportation policy, my effort is focused upon economic competitiveness in the global marketplace of the future. It is my sincere hope that someone will author a work on the social justice of U.S. transportation policy and the manner in which such transportation could and should be provided. It is my sincere hope that considering only the economics of transportation will not cloud the need for equal access to transportation for all citizens.

1

Government's view of the economy could be summed up in a few short phrases: If it moves, tax it. If it keeps moving, regulate it. And if it stops moving, subsidize it.

—*Ronald Reagan*

SYNTHESIS OF TRANSPORTATION AND ECONOMIC VITALITY

Transportation systems are the arteries and capillaries of the economic body. Whether a commuter is using mass transit, a tractor-trailer is hauling produce, a real estate agent is going to a home showing, or a parent is delivering children to school, transportation is essential to our modern life style and quality of life. Transportation is so readily available that it is nearly invisible. Day after day we use transportation systems with little consideration of how they are provided or whether they are sufficient for the entire community. However, rising congestion has raised concern that our current methods of managing and funding transportation are inadequate. Coincidently, technological revolutions in transportation are fostering new approaches and the stage is set for bold new methods of providing and pricing this critical public good.

Transportation is frequently and simply defined as the movement of people and goods. However, transporting a good changes its value and creates value where it did not previously exist. Similarly, transportation of people for the purpose of providing a service also creates economic value. This is particularly significant in the United States where 80 per cent of the Gross Domestic Product is a result of services rather than industry or agriculture[1]. The link between economic health and transportation is defined by this relationship.

Similar relationships are at the core of our quality of life. Transportation is more than a mechanism for moving from point A to point B. It allows the convenience and freedom to conveniently access recreational facilities, pick up the children at school, go shopping, visit our extended families, and travel to work. Just as access to transportation empowers, the lack of transportation can disenfranchise an individual from society. Access to jobs, education, church and other fundamental freedoms are jeopardized by transportation systems that are inaccessible or inadequate.

The Reign of the Automobile

In the United States, access to transportation nearly equates to automobile access and ownership. There are 1.1 vehicles for every licensed driver in the United States today, up from .7 per licensed driver in 1969[2] and this trend has been consistent for the last thirty years. In some of the larger cities of the United States mass transit is widely available and automobile ownership is not universal, but it is rare for a family not to own an automobile. From 1960 to 2000 the percentage of work trips made by public transit fell from 12.6 per cent to 4.7 per cent and the number of autos and light trucks per 1000 people rose from 340 to 766, resulting in the highest rate of personal vehicle ownership in the world.[3] This is about 50 per cent higher than most Western European countries.

In the fourth of a series of articles produced for the Transportation Quarterly, titled "Socioeconomics of Urban Travel: Evidence From the 2001 National Household Transportation Survey", professors John Pucher and John Renne concluded the following:

> The 2001 Nationwide Household Transportation Survey confirms most of the same travel trends and variations among socioeconomic groups documented by its predecessors, the Nationwide Personal Transportation Surveys of 1969, 1977, 1983, 1990, and 1995. The private car continues to dominate urban travel among every segment of the American population, including the poor, minorities, and the elderly. By comparison, public transport accounts for less than 2 per cent of all urban travel. Even the lowest-income households make only 5 per cent of their trips by transit.[4]

There is also a mystique to the private automobile that is worldwide. The song "Born to be Wild" typifies this mystique with the lyrics: "head out on the highway", "looking for adventure", "whatever comes my way" etc. The song reminds us of the wind blowing through our hair as we motor down the highway going, perhaps, nowhere in particular. Or, as sociologist Dr. Jim Wright describes it in his book about NASCAR,

> *"Many commentators have written about America's love affair with cars. But "love affair" hardly captures our hot, lustful, passionate fixation, an obsession really, with these mechanical Chariots of Fire. Cars embody, express and even enable all the great American values: freedom ("the faster I go, the freer I feel"), mobility, independence, self-sufficiency, status, leisure, control, speed, mastery, sensuality, affluence, power. Is this not what cars are all about? What America is all about?"[5]*

Such freedom and convenience in our lives seems worth the considerable personal capital investment and operating costs necessary to own an automobile. In other countries of the world where taxation policies make it much more costly to own and operate a personal vehicle, individuals are willing to pay a year's salary to purchase an automobile. On a trip to Oslo, Norway with the Executive Committee of the International Bridge, Tunnel and Turnpike Association (IBTTA), one of our Norwegian hosts was discussing the recent purchase of an American sport utility vehicle. He paid $25,000 US for the vehicle and almost $50,000 US for tax due at the time of purchase. His gross annual income was about 25% higher than the total cost of the vehicle. This is in a city that has excellent light rail, ring toll roads that prevent entry into Oslo without paying a toll and one of the highest gasoline tax rates in Europe. Research on developing countries indicates that the preference to own an automobile may exceed several times an individual's annual salary. The freedom represented by the automobile is not a wholly American phenomenon but is worldwide. Access to transportation is inherent to individual and national economic welfare.

The Relationship of Transportation and the Economy

The American Association of Highway and Transportation Officials (AASHTO) supported research to assess the impact that increasing traffic congestion has on economic growth. Detailed microeconomic data on business location patterns, patterns of commuting, truck trips, and other business travel patterns for the case study areas of Chicago and Philadelphia, were analyzed. Through an analysis of increased costs related to inventory, logistics and production, and ultimately the effect of higher commuting and shipping costs on business productivity, the research was able to isolate the direct effect transportation has on economic growth. The research, conducted by the National Research Council, found that a reduction of 10 per cent in travel times, which equates to a 2.5 per cent reduction of travel costs, had an annual economic impact of $980 million for the Chicago area and $240 million for the Philadelphia area.[6] These are the effects for just two cities. Imagine the economic impact if travel times could be reduced 10 per cent in all of the major metropolitan areas of the United States. Conversely, if travel times increase 10 per cent because of increased congestion, a multi-billion dollar negative economic impact results. The realization that congestion is a growing threat to the economy is well founded. Compounding the problem, congestion is not a linear phenomenon but increases geometrically.

Research performed at the University of Washington considered the relationship of congestion and economic growth and concluded that productivity of capital and labor is affected by two measures of congestion, aggregate congestion and relative congestion. Aggregate congestion is defined as an indirect service such as fire or police protection, whereas relative congestion is defined in this research as the direct use of the highway. Congestion definitions aside, it is clear that the conclusions of the study further support a relationship between transportation and the economy. The specific conclusions were:

> "Congestion, returns to scale and economic growth are intimately related economic variables" and "Aggregate congestion reduces the effective productivity of capital while relative congestion reduces the effective productivity of labor."[7]

Another researcher, David Aschauer in two articles published in 1989, found "the relationship between public investment and — productivity of private capital to be strongly positive."[8] These seminal research efforts began a debate that led to empirical research conducted by the National Cooperative Highway Research Program, which confirmed the relationship.[9]

The Impact of Trucks on the Economy

Not surprising to anyone who has traveled on the arterial highway system recently, the movement of freight by truck has grown significantly and adds to the growing congestion problem. The movement of goods is integral to the economy. Most everything around us is transported by some means. For example, on an average day, approximately 12 million pounds of food are transported into New York City: 53,600 pounds of butter, 2.2 million pounds of meat, poultry or fish, 1,340,000 pounds of fruits and juices, 3.3 million pounds of milk and cream, one million pounds of potatoes, one million pounds of sugar and sweeteners and 1.4 million pounds of flour and cereals.[10] The vast majority of this produce arrives via the flexible rubber-tire vehicle. Imagine the tons of freight related to other industries, such as office goods, paper, furniture, and electronic equipment. Once goods are consumed, the waste of consumption must then be transported out of the city core. On average, there are approximately 4.5 pounds of refuse produced daily for every person in the United States.[11] The population of New York City, not including the surrounding boroughs, was approximately 8 million in 2000; the daily refuse removal would have been 36 million pounds or 18,000 tons. The transport of food products, waste and other freight occurs on increasingly congested highways. This congested condition results in longer transport times and stimulates the addition of yet more trucks to handle the demand. Each year more vehicles travel the nation's highways just to meet existing levels of economic activity without accounting for any economic growth. These events represent an introduced inefficiency in economic impact.

Research addressing freight movement is particularly revealing. Recent information concerning the relationship between traffic congestion and economic growth was prepared by the Road Information Program in Washington, D.C. The report, published in May 2001 provides the following overall assessment.[12]

"The ability of the country's transportation system to move goods and services in an effective and cost-efficient manner is critical to the maintenance of the high standard of living enjoyed by Americans. The United States is rapidly converting to an economic structure that requires both higher levels and greater reliability of freight transport, for business-to-business and business to customer exchanges. Roads and bridges will continue to play a central role in freight transport, since most goods and services used on a daily basis are transported via the highway transportation system."

Some of the specific conclusions from that report are as follows:

The increasing use of "just-in-time" delivery techniques have made trucks rolling warehouses and made businesses increasingly dependent on reliable goods movement in and out of urban areas.

The North American Free Trade Agreement (NAFTA) has led to increased freight transport in major urban areas in the United States

72 percent of the estimated $7 trillion worth of goods shipped from sites nationwide is transported on trucks. An additional 12 percent is transported by courier services, bringing the total to 84 percent of all goods shipped that travel over roads.

From 1980 to 2000, our nation's Gross Domestic Product (GDP) increased by 86 percent. At the same time, highway travel increased by 76 percent—with the two showing similar rates of increase year by year.

Increasing traffic congestion nationwide threatens our future standard of living because the health of the economy is increasingly tied to the efficiency of goods movement across the country, largely on roads and highways.

Commercial truck travel increased by more than 37 percent from 1990 to 1999, from 96 billion miles of travel in 1990 to 132 billion miles of travel nearly a decade later.

The United States Department of Transportation projects that freight deliveries will double in most regions of the country by 2020. Moreover, 82 percent of the anticipated new goods and products shipments will be by trucks that will travel over an increasingly congested road system.

The United States is losing its traditional economic advantage of superior goods movement compared to the rest of the world because traffic congestion is reducing the efficiency of goods movement.

The report also documents the relationship between gross domestic product (GDP) and vehicular traffic. The graph below represents a twenty-year curve of total vehicle miles of travel overlaid with a plot of the GDP of the United States. The result is a pair of curves that are a near perfect fit. Clearly a relationship exists between total vehicular traffic (including all vehicles and trucks) in the United States and the GDP, a classic measure of economic output.

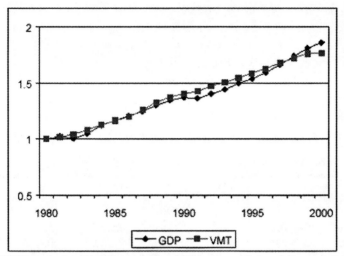

Source: TRIP analysis of U.S. Departments of Transportation and Commerce data

Figure 1: Comparison of United States Gross Domestic Product and
Vehicle Miles of Travel Growth 1980 to 2000, 1=100 percent of 1980
(adjusted for inflation)

Growth in interstate truck traffic is projected to increase in the next twenty years. By 2020 it is estimated that 60 per cent of the urban interstate mileage and 35 per cent of the rural interstate mileage will carry 10,000 trucks or more per day.[13] Also, by 2020, 90 per cent of the urban interstates will be at or near capacity.[14] The presence of 10,000 trucks per day on congested highways in a mix with smaller and more maneuverable automobiles is a safety concern for both vehicles. Without additional capacity being added to these throughways of America, logistics costs will rise, safety will deteriorate and the economy will be negatively impacted. Some have suggested that special truck lanes be provided for more efficient and safe movement of freight, especially in urban areas.

Research studies performed at the state level paint a similar picture. Local studies in Florida prepared by consultants to the Florida Transportation Commission calculated a direct cost for large commercial tractor-trailers at $1 for each minute the vehicle is idled in traffic.[15] Considering the 2 to 5 per cent profit margins on a tractor-trailer load in the United States, vehicles involved in the movement of commercial goods cannot be delayed for long or profit for the entire trip is lost.

There is further loss when one considers "just-in-time" inventory operations. Everything around us, from raw materials that have to reach the manufacturer's plant locations to the distribution of final products, is moved through the transportation system. While it is true that larger volume, bulk commodities (coal, minerals, grains etc.), are typically moved by water or rail, many of the goods and raw materials in the United States are moved across the nation's highways.

The following table provides some guidance as to those goods moved by rubber tire and, therefore, compete with passenger vehicles for highway capacity.[16]

Table 1: Commercial Freight Activity in the United States by Mode 1993 and 2002

Mode of Trans.	1993			2002		
	Value Bil. ($ 2000)	Tons millions	Ton-miles billions	Value Bil. ($ 2000)	Tons millions	Ton-miles billions
Truck	4,684	7,275	931	6,660	9,197	1,449
Rail	278	1,580	965	388	1,895	1,254
Water	620	2,128	883	867	2,345	733
Air	395	7	9	777	10	15
Pipeline	312	1,595	593	285	1,656	753
Multimodal	665	231	166	1,111	213	226
Other/ unknown	243	541	93	373	499	77
total	5,862	9,688	2,421	8,468	11,573	3,204
total-multimodal	5,197	9,458	2,255	7,358	11,359	2,978
% truck	0.901	0.769	0.413	0.905	0.810	0.486

The table shows the freight activity by mode in the United States. The total is adjusted for multimodal freight activity since part of that movement involves trucks as well. Several facts stand out from the table. First, in both 1993 and 2002 trucks carried 90 per cent of the value of all goods shipped in the United States, 75-80 per cent of the total tonnage, and 41-49 per cent of the total ton-miles. Secondly, in the short period from 1993 to 2002 a 26 per cent increase in shipment weight occurred for truck transport. This represents a significant growth in less than a decade and is evidence of the hyperactivity occurring in the truck freight industry in the United States.

Growth in truck freight movement in the U.S. is primarily the result of three events: deregulation, the North American Free Trade Agreement (NAFTA) and just-in-time inventory business practices but there are inherent factors affecting the growth of highway freight traffic as well.

Primarily, truck operations are more flexible than other modes such as rail and water. Trucks can travel door-to-door and consequently require fewer transfers of goods between modes or the need to store goods in a warehouse in the interim. This greater flexibility offered by the tractor-trailer combination versus rail or water provides the customer with the least total shipping time. While water transport is most efficient in terms of energy required to move a given weight of freight, followed by rail, the highway offers flexibility. Figure 2 below shows the relative efficiency of various modes represented as the number of miles that one ton can be moved with one gallon of fuel.[17]

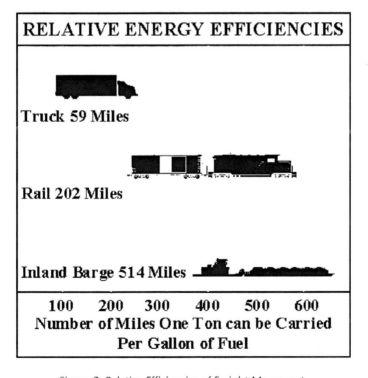

Figure 2: Relative Efficiencies of Freight Movement

From strictly an efficiency perspective, inland barges are ten times more efficient that a tractor-trailer and rail is about four times as efficient. However, if a navigable waterway does not exist near the beginning and the end of a freight transit, transfers will be required to other modes requiring a great deal of logistical support resulting in a longer trip time. Likewise, a railhead or rail spur must exist for rail to compete with the highway and the loads must be easily divisible for loading and easily broken down for distribution. Rarely does rail operate door-to-door. It is common for freight to be transferred between rail and trucks at either the origin or near the destination of the trip. Further, rail cars are formed into trains for transit and in the process are assembled, disassembled and then reassembled to form new train sets. This may happen several times during transit from origin to final destination and such yard activity can add significantly to the total door-to-door shipment time.

The flexibility offered by the highway even draws bulk freight. In today's world, a two-person driving team can take a 40 ton tractor-trailer combination across the three-thousand-mile expanse of America in a work week, and pick up and deliver door to door. "Just-in-time" business operations thrive on such efficiency. The resulting economic power generated is dependent upon an uncongested highway system and nonstop operations. The interstate highway system has been such a system.

The Interstate Highway System

The construction of America's interstate highway system was the largest public works project in the history of the world. The 42,700-mile[18] long system allows nonstop travel to all major urban areas of the United States and many rural areas. The construction of the system began in 1956 with the passage of legislation designating the National Defense Highway System. While much can be said about the destructive cultural, environmental and societal impacts of the Interstate system, the network has had enormously positive economic benefits. The interstate system passed with a total appropriation of $25 billion for the period 1957 through 1969.[19] The system was near completion in 1995 and through that year the total cost of the system had reached $350 billion. In 1957 dollars the total would have been $58.5 billion.[20] In effect, the nation passed a bill valued at $58.5 billion when the total federal budget for the same year was $93.7 billion. The passage of this legislation was a bold initiative. Funding was to be via the federal gasoline tax.

The system was originally defined in 1947 to be 40,000 miles in length and was to be completed in 1972. On June 29, 1956, President Eisenhower signed the Federal Aid Highway Act, which authorized 41,000 miles. From 1956 until 1975 approximately 1,500 miles were added to the definition and the system was declared complete in 1992. Many of the additional miles were the result of congress "bringing home the bacon" in the form of urban beltways. These additions were "manna from heaven" for the urban areas. The funding was 90 percent federal and 10 percent state. While no local money was required, enormous local economic benefit resulted. The system was intended to be an interstate system and the beltways were for bypassing the central business districts, but in many urban areas the system came to be used predominantly for local trips and generated expanded urban development. The use patterns altered the system's purpose from "interstate" to urban arterial.

The interstate highway system is a fully controlled access system that precludes "at-grade" access and intersections with stop signs and traffic signals. Such a system provides uninterrupted, high-volume capacity. Because it was to be a high-speed expressway, standards for interchange spacing were defined by the USDOT and strict control on the frequency of Interstate interchanges resulted. Depicted below is a typical urban interchange on the interstate system.

The interstate system provides a theoretical capacity of 2,200 vehicles per hour per lane or 8,800 vehicles per hour in both directions for a typical four-lane section. Other urban arterial highway systems with signalized intersections and many business accesses provide much less capacity. Many variables affect the ultimate capacity of these other urban arterial highways such as the frequency of median cuts for left turns into businesses, the frequency of right turn business access curb cuts, and the frequency and timing of signalized intersections. Generally, an urban highway will provide approximately 1,200 vehicles per hour per lane, or about half the capacity of a fully controlled access interstate or expressway. Further, an interstate highway will retain capacity over the life of the project since the frequency of interchanges is regulated by the federal government and is less subject to local political pressures to allow business access. Contrasted to "at grade" facilities, a fully controlled access roadway, like the interstate is similar to the arteries of the human body, and state, city and county streets are similar to capillaries that connect to the remote parts of the body. The interstate highway system is the economic envy of the world. It is this highway system that has supported the enormous post war economic growth and catalyzed our economic prosperity.

NAFTA and Deregulation

Truck freight delivery growth resulting from just-in-time inventory control has been amplified with the advent of two momentous and near simultaneous events: the North American Free Trade Agreement and the deregulation of the trucking industry.

President Clinton signed the NAFTA agreement between Canada, the United States and Mexico into law on December 8, 1993. The primary purpose was to eliminate tariff and non-tariff barriers to free trade within ten years and to open up new investment opportunities in key sectors. The Canada-United States trade relationship is the largest between any two nations of the globe. Two-way trade in goods and services between Canada and the United States during 2000 was estimated at approximately C$700 billion, or almost C$2 billion per day.[21] Mexico is now the second largest trading partner with the United States. The enormous trade growth with Mexico and Canada has been a direct result of NAFTA.

Concurrent with this growth in trade in North America, the trucking industry was being deregulated. The federal government began regulating prices in interstate commerce in 1887 with the formation of the Interstate Commerce Commission, ICC. Initially regulation was focused on railroad transport to prevent monopolistic practices. Trucking was included in 1935 after heavy lobbying by state regulators, railroads, and the ICC itself. The law required motor carriers to file freight rates with the ICC before they were allowed to become effective, including the establishment of a new route. Anyone was allowed to inspect the proposed pricing, including competing railroads or competing trucking companies. Until 1980, when partial deregulation occurred, it was almost impossible to add a route unless no one was opposed. Therefore purchasing corridor rights from existing operators was the only practical method to enter the market. Studies in the United States and abroad demonstrate that regulation has had the effect of increasing freight rates significantly, which in turn has an effect on the economies of those countries. Studies in the U.S. show that transport rates for products exempt from ICC regulation were 20 to 40 percent less than those for the same products under regulation.[22] Studies performed comparing regulated countries such as the United States and West Germany to unregulated Great Britain revealed that rates were 75 percent higher in regulated countries.

Deregulation has been a tremendous boost to the economic vitality of the United States. Deregulation began in 1977, and in the subsequent five years rates decreased 25 percent and revenue per ton fell 22 percent with increases in service quality.[23] These events made the truck an even more attractive alternative for hauling freight and generated significant growth in truck traffic. In one decade, 1980 to 1990, the number of licensed carriers doubled to a total of 40,000.

Deregulation and just-in-time inventory was happening simultaneously and each had its effect on the other. A significant economic gain resulted from the deregulation of the trucking industry but the greater flexibility provided by deregulation also contributed to the new inventory methods and the shift in freight logistics. During this period a substantial reduction in the cost of ware-housing and maintaining inventories occurred because truckers were better able to provide flexible, on-time service, allowing just-in-time manufacturing and retailing. Concurrently, profit margins for freight transportation were driven to historic lows as the independent and freedom-loving trucker took to the wide-open spaces of America's highways. As a result of NAFTA, deregulation and just-in-time business strategies, trucking plays an even more crucial role in the relationship of transportation to the economy. The inventories that once existed at factories and retailing locations are now traveling the highways destined to arrive at a specific time and place.

While research and data are conclusive about the transportation/economic relationship, there are also theoretical underpinnings that amplify our under-standing and are consistent with the changes in freight logistics that have occurred. The concepts of time and place utility are fundamental and provide a backdrop for understanding freight transportation efficiency and the adequacy of our transportation systems.

A Theoretical Framework

Time utility theory states that the value of a good is partially based upon its time of delivery or availability. For example, raw materials for manufacturing or component parts in an assembly process have a different value depending upon when they arrive. Materials arriving months ahead of time require investment in storage, accounting, warehousing equipment, financial carrying costs, etc. They are, therefore, of less value if delivered too far in advance. If delivered too late, the costs can be enormous. Entire assembly lines can be idled while awaiting the arrival of components. Analyses of time utility have led many companies to adopt just-in-time inventory methods in order to compete in a reduced cost structure. The manufacturing component and retail inventories of yester-year are today in transit, somewhere in the transportation system, usually on tractor-trailers competing for limited transportation capacity.

Retail operations have also altered standard business practices to improve efficiency and the result has been nothing short of revolutionary. Rather than pushing inventory through the system to the consumer, goods are now pulled through the system. In traditional "push" methods, products are produced, stored in a warehouse, and the retail sector pushes to sell the inventory, sometimes through extensive discounting methods. The "pull" concept of inventory management in retail works in reverse. Retailers prescribe the number of units to be produced and delivered to the retail locations and at precise times. Reduced inventory and commensurate cost reductions have made retailing very competitive and those who have been slow to modify practices have experienced large reductions in market share, some to the point of business failure. Just like the warehouse inventories of component parts used in manufacturing, warehouse inventories of completed products have reduced.

Services are impacted by surface transportation as well. The economic value of services can also be defined by time utility. For a service to have value it must arrive on schedule, much like assembly line components and retail products. Consider a consultant who arrives at an important corporate client meeting after the meeting has ended or a bid document that arrives at 5:05 p.m. when it is due at precisely 5:00 p.m. If it arrives at 4:59 p.m. and is the low bid, the document is valued at the amount of the contract, but the same document has no value if it arrives after 5:00 p.m. regardless of the bid amount.

Services that require special expertise and must be performed in the presence of the client are especially time sensitive. Even services that do not necessarily require the presence of the customer such as lawn services, pest control, etc. have a time limit before the customer chooses to use another service. Traffic congestion levels in urban areas particularly affect the costs of providing these services. I recall a particularly salient presentation by the CEO of a large pest control company describing how congestion directly related to the need for more trucks and people to handle the same workload as the previous year because of increases in traffic congestion.

These examples demonstrate the critical nature of dispatch and tracking systems in today's transportation systems. The examples also provide some enlightenment as to why the Internet thrives in a services based economy. Information and transportation systems have become inextricably linked and interdependent. As a corollary, information has become more valuable and the competition for information can be the deciding factor between surviving and thriving. Information about the instantaneous location of goods in transit, approximate arrival times, etc., play an ever increasing role in the economy, especially considering the time utility of the transaction.

Just as the value of a product is the sum of production cost, transportation and profit a similar equation holds for the value of an hour of service. The wage cost plus overhead, expenses and profit make up the value of an hour of service. In an economy in which services account for a large proportion of the GNP, transportation and telecommunications can be the determining factor in profitability.

The companion concept to time utility is place utility. Simply stated, the value of a good or service is directly related to its location. An orange in Florida has less value than the same orange in the same condition located in Saskatchewan, Canada simply because of the large number of oranges grown in Florida versus Saskatchewan. Transportation adds value by changing the location of the product. Consider a supply demand chart for oranges in Florida and one in Saskatchewan. They would be quite different in terms of price derived in the respective locations and transportation provides the means for balancing these market differences. If, however, the cost of transportation exceeds the value added to the goods, the product will not be transported to the locale that would generate the higher price. If the absence of oranges in Saskatchewan continues over time, the price will rise until the cost of transportation is justified and the oranges are transported. All of this assumes a perfect provision of information by all parties in the transaction.

The concept of place utility also holds in a service economy. Consider a surgeon trained to perform a unique procedure. A patient who requires that procedure would place an enormous value on the services of the surgeon. However, if there is no way to transport the surgeon to the patient or vice versa, the value of the services to that patient, are zero. Today this particular service commodity is beginning to be provided without the physical transportation of either the patient or the surgeon.

Telecommunications and the Internet are changing service relationships and the performance of services. In the case of the surgeon, sophisticated robotic surgical equipment connected via telecommunication lines can perform remote surgery. Though technically possible, various cultural and psychological aspects of surgery can play a deciding role.

While many specialized services can be performed via modern telecommunications, there are social and business perspectives that sometimes require personal contact. For example, personal interaction is sometimes necessary if professional credibility is to be maintained. Such a practice can provide a competitive advantage. For example, would you be most likely to purchase a home from a real estate agent that joins you on visits to properties or from one who provides the listing of properties online. Certainly, the Internet provides added value to the provision of services but the Internet and telecommunications are frequently insufficient as a substitute for personal service.

Information as a Catalyst to Efficiency

The provision of information can be of tremendous importance though it is rare that information is a complete substitute for transportation. However, there are instances where this could happen. Consider the case of two trucks filling orders for the transportation of oranges, one from Orlando to Jacksonville and one from Jacksonville to Orlando. If perfect communications and information existed, the trips would not take place. In such a case, information directly substitutes for transportation. When information replaces the movement of goods or someone attempting to provide a service, the value added by transportation is zero. The substitution of information for transportation occurs more frequently as information systems improve, but more often information is supplementary to transportation.

Freight efficiency is however being greatly improved by the provision of information. Matching loads to tractor trailer combinations is a common example of information supplementing transportation. The information prevents tractor operators from having to "deadhead" back to a location where they can pick up a trailer and allows trucking fleets to optimize efficiency on the loads assigned. Independent carriers also subscribe to these information services.

Information affects economic segments in varying ways. In addition to the movement of goods, services benefit economically from the information age. In fact, some areas of the service economy are restructuring as a result of the provision of information. Examples include mortgage financing, automobile retailing and libraries to name a few.

Research clearly establishes the relationship between the adequacy of transportation systems and economic vitality and the highway system is the transportation mode most influential, particularly the controlled access Interstate and expressway systems. Various statutory and regulatory policies have caused a greater proportion of freight to be transported by truck and the automobile and light duty truck continue to be the primary transportation mode for the services sector. The theories of time and place utility broaden our understanding of this relationship and a review of national transportation and economic data will provide conclusive evidence of the relationship. Historical events demonstrate conforming aberrations of economic vitality and major transportation initiatives. When viewed in a comparative analysis with other nations, the data once again confirm the close relationship between transportation and economic growth. Each of these analyzes will be explored.

Comparative National Economic Data

What role does transportation perform on a macroeconomic level in making a nation economically competitive? Do the inherent economics of a nation define transportation system composition? For example, nations whose economies are based on processing natural resources for export, such as petroleum, would be expected to possess a pipeline transportation system and deep water ports for exporting petroleum to the world market. For nations whose economy is based on services, the relationship is less clear and mature economies tend to generate more economic value from services than from industry or agriculture. The reverse is true for developing nations. Mature nations also tend to exhibit a broad-based economy and it is more difficult to confirm a relationship of economic growth based on transportation mode. What is clear from comparative national data, however, is that transportation infrastructure stimulates economic growth.

Data from the U.S. Central Intelligence Agency, The World Factbook provides some enlightening comparative national data[24], Table 2 is an excerpt of data from that site and represent economies that are predominantly goods based, services based, and those that represent a balanced economy. The data demonstrate the relationship between transportation and economic development. Calculations are performed to show economic information on a per-mile or per capita basis.

Table 2. Transportation and Economic Data on Selected Nations

	Venezuela	Switzerland	U.S.	Germany	Japan	China
Land Sq Km	882	39.9	9,159	349	375	9,326
Pop. (MM)	24.3	7.3	281	83.3	127.0	1.284
GDP	$146.2 B	$231 B	$10.082 T	$2.184 T	$3.55 T	$6 T
GDP(T)/ Capita	$6.1	$31.7	$36.3	$26.6	$28.0	$4.6

Table 2. Transportation and Economic Data on Selected Nations (Continued)

	Venezuela	Switzerland	U.S.	Germany	Japan	China
% Agri-culture	5%	2%	2%	1%	1%	18%
% Indus-try	40%	34%	18%	31%	31%	49%
% Ser-vices	55%	64%	80%	68%	68%	33%
Km Paved (T)	32.3	71.1	5,733.0	650.9	863.0	271.3
Km Paved/1k	1.33	9.73	20.43	7.82	6.80	0.21
Km Rail(T)	.7	4.4	212.4	48.0	23.6	67.5
Km Rail/ 1k	0.028	0.60	0.76	0.58	0.19	0.052
Number Ports	13	1	22	16	21	20
Km pipe-line/1k	0.45	.25	.76	.027	.017	0.015
Km water-ways	7.1	.065	41.0	7.5	1.8	110.0

Venezuela was selected to show the relationship between the development of the nation's pipeline and seaport facilities and the economy based on petroleum exports while China, Germany and Japan were selected for relative total economic output and to provide comparisons to the United States. The data seem to confirm that service based economies result more from economic maturity than industrial history.

Venezuela is a fascinating example of transportation modal development and economic growth. The economy is almost singularly based on the production of the predominant commodity, petroleum. The petroleum sector dominates the economy, accounting for roughly a third of GDP, around 80 per cent of export earnings, and more than half of government operating revenues.[25] It is extremely fortunate that Venezuela has the geography to support deep-water ports. These ports provide for a very efficient form of transportation, ocean going oil tankers which move the raw petroleum to refining locations or the final refined product to importing nations.

A contrast between Venezuela and the U.S. is immediately evident. Venezuela has 1.33 kilometers of paved road per thousand population while the United States has 20.43. Venezuela has .45 kilometers of pipeline per thousand population and 2/3 as many deep water ports as the United States, which has a GDP 69 times the size of Venezuela. Obviously, the Venezuelan pipeline system is well developed but the U.S. has more pipeline per capita than even Venezuela. While lacking in profundity, these data are quite important in demonstrating the close relationship between the economies and transportation systems of these nations.

The data also further demonstrate the relationship between the degree to which the transportation system is developed and the economic output of the country. This is particularly evident for the United States. The U.S. is the largest single economy in the world and it also has more railway kilometers per thousand population and more kilometers of paved roads per thousand population than any of the nations shown in the table. The U.S. has more paved kilometers in absolute terms and on a per capita basis than any of the countries listed and the same is true for rail infrastructure investment. Over the last century and a half the U.S. has made enormous investments in transportation infrastructure. Just as this investment has provided economic benefit, the maintenance of this investment and additions to the investment will be required to support future economic growth. If such investments cease, economic impacts will be the inevitable result. Though these impacts may not occur until after several political election cycles, they will occur and the ability to reverse the momentum of inadequate investment policy will become more protracted with each passing year.

The data clearly indicate what a powerhouse the United States economy is and the breadth of the intermodal transportation system in America. As Table 2 shows, the United States has more kilometers of pipeline per thousand population than Venezuela, whose economy is dependent upon petroleum production. This country has more paved road per thousand population than any of the developed or developing countries by a factor of two. Rail mileage per thousand population is closer to other developed countries. Clearly, the United States transportation system is second to none. This phenomenon can be partially explained by the expansive geography of the United States and the greater degree of suburbanization but these comparisons continue even when measured on a per capita basis.

As would be expected, developing nations possess significantly less transportation infrastructure than developed nations. China and the United States are stark contrasts to one another. While of similar land size (Alaska is included in the United States data), the United States has 100 times the paved roadway per thousand population contrasted to China and ten times the railway kilometers measured to population.

The developmental status of a nation is also exhibited in the percentage of the GDP generated by agriculture, industry and services. Those nations with the greater developmental status have more GDP generated by industry and services rather than agriculture. The United States, generates 80 per cent of its GDP through the provision of services.

National comparative data verifies the link between the transportation infrastructure and economic development and conclusively establishes the leadership position that the United States has had in surface transportation.

Historical Perspective—Roman Roads

The history of transportation also provides some insight into the relationship between transportation and the economy. There are many examples of ancient world transportation systems but the transportation network of the Roman Empire is especially demonstrative. The roadway network of the Roman Empire clearly demonstrates the nexus between the transportation system and economic power. At the peak of economic and military power, the paved roads of the ancient Roman Empire encompassed more than 50,000 miles stretching from Britain to Mesopotamia and were further supported by another 200,000 miles of unpaved roads.[26] The major population centers were connected via this network and cities sprang up from the intersections of major thoroughfares that still exist today. Many of these roadways still exist today and are part of the modern European roadway network. The system was complemented with extraordinary access by water, and together provided the network by which trade of the known world was conducted.

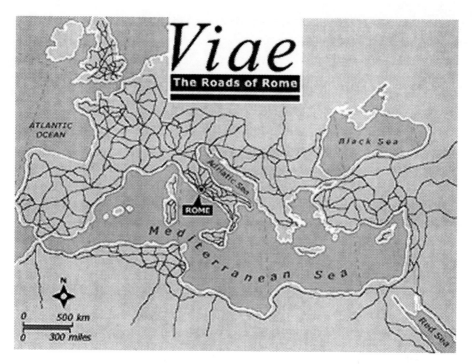

Illustration 1: The Ancient Roadway Network of the Roman Empire

Various modes of transportation can be critical to the development of a society economically and socially. We think of issues of economic growth and quality of life today but these issues have always been important and related to surface transportation. The roadway system of the Roman Empire certainly served these purposes but there were other surface transportation modes that were important to economic and societal goals. A crucial economic and life-sustaining product that must be transported for any society is water. The Romans were adept at moving water through gravity-fed pipelines and aqueducts. The aqueducts allowed Roman cities to grow to populations not previously possible and some of these structures were 90 kilometers in length. Historical research confirms that ancient Rome delivered about 70 liters of water per capita to its citizens on a daily basis. By comparison to the United States per capita consumption today is about 250 liters per day, this is an astounding statistic.[27] Though the roman system provided a continuous flow versus the on demand flow of a modern society, the comparison is amazing. With the provision of this critical resource, Roman cities could support populations of nearly 1 million people. The development of this network to transmit water further demonstrates the intimate relationship between transportation and the economy.

Historical Perspective—Western Europe and Russia

The 20th century in Europe offers more examples of the relationship of economic power to transportation system development. The European countries of Germany, France and Italy offer some interesting insights. These countries are somewhat similar in land area and economic development and experienced vast upheaval during the first and second world wars. Similarly, the economic growth of these countries was coincident with the reconstruction of the transportation facilities destroyed.

Table 3: Trans. and Economic Data, Western Europe, Russia, and U.S.

	France	Italy	UK	Germany	US	Japan	Russia
Pop 1k	60,181	57,998	60,095	82,398	290,343	127,214	144,526
Area sq km(T)	545.6	294.0	241.6	349.2	9,158.96	374.75	16,995.80
Road km(T)	894.0	479.7	371.9	230.8	3,737.6	534.5	358.8
Xway km	11,500	6,621	3,358	11,515	89,426	6,455	NA
Rail km	32,682	19,493	16,893	45,514	194,731	23,168	87,157
GNP (trillions)	1.56	1.46	1.53	2.16	10.45	3.65	1.41
Road/1000cap	14.855	8.271	6.189	2.800	12.873	4.201	2.483
Xway/100cap	1.911	1.142	0.559	1.397	3.080	0.507	NA
Rail/100cap	5.431	3.361	2.811	5.524	6.707	1.821	6.031
Area/road	0.6	0.6129	0.6496	1.5135	2.4505	0.7011	47.3641
Area/xway	47.4	44.4072	71.9446	30.3277	102.4194	58.0548	NA
Area/rail	16.7	15.0834	14.3012	7.6729	47.0339	16.1751	195.0021
GNP/road MM	$1.74	$3.03	$4.11	$9.36	$2.80	$6.83	$3.93

Table 3: Trans. and Economic Data, Western Europe, Russia, and U.S. (Continued)

	France	Italy	UK	Germany	US	Japan	Russia
GNP/xway MM	$135.48	$219.76	$455.03	$187.58	$116.86	$565.61	NA
GNP/rail MM	$47.67	$74.64	$90.45	$47.46	$53.66	$157.59	$16.17
GNP/cap MM	$25.89	$25.09	$25.43	$26.21	$35.99	$28.70	$9.75

Russia stands in striking contrast to the European community. Russian land area dwarfs the European countries and the population is somewhat larger. The much larger distances between major economic centers is further complicated by the less developed transportation system and, to an extent, climatic conditions. The strategy of the Soviet military during World War II incorporated the factors of geography, weather and transportation into a winning military strategy. With the advance of the German military the Soviets destroyed any food or war-making resources, thereby lengthening the German supply lines. Further, the railroad gage in the Soviet Union was different from the European gage making it more difficult to transport military goods. Transportation therefore played a key role in the Soviet ability to withstand invasion.

Whether measured before or after World War II, Russia had a much lower capability to move people and goods. Postwar Russia had great difficulty providing food for its population, partially due to the failure of collectivism in agriculture and partially due to the farm-to-market transportation system. In postwar Russia fully one half of farm products perished in transit to the marketplace.[28] Half the food supply came from small peasant garden plots, most of which were located on the huge government-run collective farms.[29] The time distances were perhaps of greater importance than the physical distances. A more poignant demonstration of time utility would be difficult to conjure. It is interesting to hypothesize how far Germany might have been able to penetrate the Soviet Empire had the transportation system been more fully developed. The Russian transportation system continues to contrast with European countries in terms of kilometers of rail and paved roadway per thousand population. The contrast is particularly evident with Germany. However, these measures of transportation development are vastly different when land area is considered. The land area of Russia is twice that of the U.S. and 32 times the land area of the next largest European country of

France. When the transportation network is viewed in comparison to the gross national product and geographic area, Russia is anomalous to its European counterparts. Russia has twenty times the land area per roadway kilometer as the U.S. and even more when compared to European countries.

Eras of Transportation in the United States

Transportation economics is further demonstrated by the history of the U.S. The history of transportation in the United States is coincident with the progress in transportation efficiency during the industrial revolution. Transportation efficiency progress is a combination of more efficient vehicles and the development of the transportation network. The developing nations of Europe and the U.S. shared in the benefits of improvements in vehicle locomotion but the public provision of roads and rails was unique to each country. Though European systems were certainly disrupted during the World Wars of the last century, they were essentially rebuilt. Also, countries like the U.S., are bordered by oceans, crisscrossed with naturally occurring navigable internal waterways and other natural features that support the development of trade routes. But these factors aside the history of the economic development of the United States coincides with investments in transportation infrastructure. Many of these investments were daring in scope and took full advantage in the improvements in vehicular efficiency.

Accepted definitions of transportation efficiency are the concepts of ton-miles for freight transportation and passenger-miles for passenger travel. The ton-mile is the effort required to move one ton over a distance of one mile or one pound 2,000 miles or two tons, ½ mile. The table below shows how ton-mile efficiency has increased with developments in locomotion.

The information in Table 4 is dated to the 1961 source of the information but nevertheless shows the exponential increases in vehicular efficiency that occurred.

Table 4: Transportation Efficiency and Progress in Locomotion[30]

Type of Carrier	Output (ton-miles/day)
Man's Back (100lb/20 mi)	1
Pack Horse (200lb/40 mi)	4
Wheelbarrow (400lb/20 mi)	4
Cart (1,000lb/20 mi)	10
Team & Wagon (3 tons/40 mi)	120

Table 4: Transportation Efficiency and Progress in Locomotion[30] (Continued)

Type of Carrier	Output (ton-miles/day)
Motor Truck (10 tons/240 mi)	2,400
Railroad (2,000 tons/40 mi)	80,000

When coupled with the development of the roadway and rail network, the ability to affect the time and place utility of goods was significantly affected. The table demonstrates that railroad transportation is the most efficient form of ground transportation, followed by tractor-trailers. All of these forms of locomotion are less efficient than water transportation. Water transportation, of course, requires a port for off-loading freight and transportation efficiency can be lost through transfers, such as occurs at seaports and rail yards. To optimize the efficiency of the total trip, transfers must be minimal.

Today, the total allowable weight of a five-axle tractor-trailer is 80,000 lbs. or 40 tons, (assuming a load average of 25 tons). If a fully loaded truck travels the interstate highways of America at 70 miles per hour, in a 10 hour day (allowing for two hours of break during the day) such a vehicle could move 14,000 ton-miles per day. This example also provides some measure of the effect that the interstate system has had on freight movement in the United States.

The chart was taken from a text prepared before the interstate highway era and offers a comparison of truck freight efficiency. Note that the average efficiency for a "motor truck" was 10 tons over 240 miles versus 25 tons over 560 miles today. The improvement in efficiency is 583 per cent. While some of this efficiency is the result of vehicle technology and deregulation, the majority is related to improvements in the highway infrastructure.

One might assume that the transportation system naturally developed as the economy expanded and vehicle efficiency dictated. However, the history of the United States is replete with major transportation projects that were extraordinary, even daring in scope and resulted in significant stimulus to the economy.

These major initiatives are roughly coincident with half century periods of development in the U.S. Some were the result of national actions to expand transportation with the motivation to tie the country together politically and economically, and to some extent, by national defense. Such was the case with the expansion of the rail network in the 19th century and the interstate highway system of the 20th century. Expansion of the roadway network in the first half of the twentieth century was predominantly in response to the invention and commercialization of the automobile but the latter half of the century was dominated by the interstate highway system.

These eras roughly coincide with half-century marks from 1850 to the present. Before the development of the modern steam engine, the most efficient method of locomotion was water transportation. During the late eighteenth century and early nineteenth century many miles of canals were constructed along major trade routes in the United States. Some of these projects were massive in scope. At one point, a canal was begun that would have stretched from Illinois through the Cumberland Gap to the East Coast. Though only portions of this canal were built, the fact that they were begun is indicative of the daring and initiative of the early U.S. leaders to construct superior, efficient transportation systems.

From the late 1700s through the 1850s land transportation in the United States was mostly dependent upon the horse. The advent of the steam engine led to the Fulton steamboat, first deployed in 1804. While horse drawn carts and wagons offered door-to-door flexibility, horse drawn barges and river rafts offered the most efficient modes of freight movement during this period. Regions that did not have navigable waterways began to construct canals to take advantage of the greater efficiency of water transit. Throughout this era, horse and wagon, water barge and steamboat composed the bulk of the country's transportation capability.

As railroads developed from the application of steam power, the steamboat era began to wane. The steamboat enjoyed a short period of prominence as the transportation vehicle of choice, but was quickly supplanted by the railroad's greater flexibility to cover the expansive land area of the U.S. The B&O railroad was active in 1830 and railways were quickly constructed, predominantly throughout the Eastern United States. The table below shows the number of miles of railroad in the United States from the inception in 1830 through modern times.

Table 5: Mileage of Railroad in the United States 1830-1995[31]

1830	23
1840	2,808
1860	30,626
1870	52,922
1880	93,267
1890	163,597

Table 5: Mileage of Railroad in the United States 1830-1995[31] (Continued)

1900	201,000
1950	223,779
1995	230,000

Clearly, enormous growth in the network happened during and after the Civil War and continued through 1900. One hundred years later, the rail network is only slightly larger than it was at the turn of the century which shows how the flexibility of the highway system offered the best total trip efficiency. During the Civil War, enormous rail system expansion occurred, and the transcontinental railroad was completed in 1869.

The story of the transcontinental railroad is a fascinating story, told with great color and excitement by the late Steven Ambrose in *Nothing Like it in the World*.[32] The method of finance is particularly noteworthy.

The construction was capitalized by granting every other section of land along the rail line to the constructor. The ownership of this property allowed the sale of bonds to the public and funds from bond sales then allowed further construction to occur and the financial process perpetuated itself. Construction continued until the Union Pacific, constructing from the east, and Central Pacific, constructing from the west met at Promontory Point, Utah, completing the transcontinental railroad. It is also interesting to note that such a phenomenal transportation project began with the passage of Pacific Railroad Act in 1862 during the Civil War and was completed on May 10, 1869.

The transcontinental link was an astounding feat. It reduced the New York to San Francisco travel time from months by boat around South America to 10 days. The economic impact of such an improvement in transit was enormous, and the daring demonstrated by the leadership of the United States is striking. There were many political reasons for tying the country together, and every president from Washington forward shared in the dream.

Consider, however, the risk of beginning construction during the Civil War. There was little available funding. Revenue was grossly insufficient, the credit market was oversold as a result of the sale of federal bonds to finance the war, and there was considerable concern about scandal in the process.

With the expansion of railroad mileage during and immediately following the Civil War, an economic expansion occurred like none before. Fueled by immigration from Europe, the United States economic course was set. Agriculture was a predominant force of economic expansion and agricultural products were assured access to markets by the expanded transportation system. During the second half of the nineteenth century the railroad reigned supreme. Rail mileage growth slowed with the turn of the century, the proliferation of the automobile and the beginning of freight hauling by truck.

The first gasoline-powered automobile was built in 1889, and the first mass production of automobiles in the United States was in 1901 and the first mass produced automobile was the Oldsmobile. The proliferation of the automobile in America was begun with the Model T Ford. Henry Ford began mass-producing the Model T in 1908 and by 1927, when it was discontinued, 18 million had been sold.[33]

With the commercial success of the automobile, a great demand for roadways developed. To fund this highway expansion, the first gas tax of two cents, was applied to gasoline in 1916. The stated purpose and justification of the tax was to finance the construction of roadways that would "get the public out of the mud." The precedent of funding highways from gasoline tax and paying for construction on a cash basis was born. This first gas tax began a thirty-year roadway construction program that lasted until World War II. This program was also used as a method for employing millions during the Great Depression. While two World Wars occurred in the first half of the century, the United States continued to add roadway mileage. It was, however, the second half of the twentieth century, with the construction of the interstate highway system that highway mileage was expanded and transportation efficiency vastly improved.

After World War II, Congress initiated the establishment of an interstate highway system. In 1952, the Federal-Aid Highway Act authorized $25 million for the interstate system. Congress passed the National Interstate and Defense Highways Act in 1956, initially defining the interstate network, and construction of the world's largest public works project began. As the twentieth century closed, the superhighway was essentially complete. As described earlier, this system of highways has had enormous economic impact, similar to that of the railways in the 19th century. This era also saw the mass commercialization of air travel in the United States. The century's last fifty years experienced enormous growth in airline passenger traffic and lightweight, high-value freight traffic. From 1980 to 2000 alone, airfreight grew from 5 billion ton-miles to 15 billion ton-miles[34], and airline passenger miles grew from 204 billion to 486 billion.[35] Long distance, high-value mobility existed as never before. Concurrently, surface transportation became dependent upon the interstate system for both freight and passengers. With the exception of long distance passenger travel and high-value freight, the vast majority of freight and passenger mobility remained linked to the highway systems and in particular the interstate highway system. The Table below shows the growth in automobile registrations from 1900 to 2000.

Table 6: United States Automobile growth in the Twentieth Century[36]

1900	8,000
1910	500,000
1923	13,000,000
1929	25,700,000
1940	27,500,000
1950	43,256,000
1960	61,671,390
1970	89,243,557
1980	121,600,843
1990	133,700,496
2000	133,621,420

It is interesting to note that there was no growth in the number of passenger cars registered in the United States in the last decade. However in that same period the number of two-axle four-tire vehicles grew from 48,274,555 in 1990 to 79,084,979 in 2000[37] clearly demonstrating the popularity of sport utility vehicles and vans in the United States.

The transportation history of the U.S. could be viewed as roughly conforming to the following fifty year increments:

Steam Development Era	1800-1850
Railroad Expansion Era	1850-1900
Highway Development Era	1900-1950
Interstate and Air Era	1950-2000

Economic results for the same periods provide interesting evidence of a cause-and-effect relationship between transportation and economic expansion. Though economic measurement is difficult to ascertain over the two centuries, some data is available.

The GNP of the nation in 1870, one year after the completion of the transcontinental railroad, was $6.7 billion,[38] the population was approximately 23 million[39], and the total of all government deficits for the years 1850 to 1900 was $991 million.[40] The twentieth century began with a surplus of $63 million with total outlays at $525 million. In that year the population was about 76 million and the number of registered automobiles from Table 4 for 1900 was 8,000. The table below shows economic data ending at each half century since 1850 and is gleaned from various historical and government sources.

Table 7: United States Population and Economic Data 1850-2000

	1850	1900	1950	2000
GNP $billions	$6.7 (1870)		$510.3	$9860.8
Pop. (millions)	23.192	75.995	151.7	281.4
U.S. Budget (millions)		$525	$42,562	$1,788,773
Deficit/Surplus ($millions)	$-991 thru 1900	$63	$3,119	$236,392

While it is difficult to obtain economic data for two centuries that supports an analysis of economic growth in relation to transportation developments, orders of magnitude indicate the economic leaps for those periods. Clearly, the United States saw enormous economic prosperity synchronously with increases in transportation mobility. Whether economic growth was the result of the transportation developments or the reverse the nexus between the two is conclusive. It is clear that such economic growth could not have happened without huge improvements in mobility as the catalyzing agent.

The challenge today is to prevent economic stagnation that results from an underinvestment in the surface transportation system. It is historically clear that economic growth is dependent upon corollary investments in transportation. A stagnation of growth in the United States should not be allowed to occur as a result of under investments in transportation and particularly ground transportation.

Urban congestion is growing at an increasing rate and rural congestion on major connecting arterials and Interstates is similarly increasing. Negative economic impact will ultimately result. The time has come to revolutionize transportation policy as a foundation for future economic growth.

The Next United States Era in Transportation

What is the next transportation era for the U.S.? If we desire a foundation for growth commensurate with that of the past, our policies must be daring and grand in scale. They must incorporate methods to take advantage of technological advances and nothing short of reinventing the United States ground transportation should be acceptable. Incremental, evolutionary approaches were not the sort of thinking that created the largest economy in the world, and will not be successful now. There is certainly a need to add highway capacity in urban areas and on some heavily traveled rural corridors as well, but to do so as "more of the same" without pricing mechanisms will result in a continuation of policy that provides surface transportation at a perceived price of zero. Such policies will perpetuate demand levels that will exceed capacity very quickly. Transportation policies must catalyze economic activity and at the same time encourage the most efficient transport of freight and passengers without unduly limiting the "invisible hand" of the marketplace.

Transportation can be funded on the premise that all should have access to a general public good or funding policies might be based on the concept that if you use the public good you pay for it, just as you would for the purchase of a private good. If transportation is considered a general public good it would be funded through some form of a general tax. In such a case, each citizen pays according to his or her income, property, vehicle cost or some other scale. However, such taxation policies do not establish a cognizant relationship between the use of a facility and the cost and therefore creates the potential for unlimited demand. A continuation of surrogate user fees, such as gasoline tax would result in a similar outcome as recent history has demonstrated. Further, the political reality of increasing such taxes to a level sufficient to fund surface transportation expansion is minimal. Meanwhile the service levels continue to deteriorate.

To stimulate the economy and affect the behavior of the transportation user, a direct relationship between use and cost must be established. The approach must, of necessity, be politically accomplishable and conscious of the potential to disenfranchise citizens that might not be able to financially participate. Because access to transportation will determine the ability of citizens to participate in economic expansion and quality of life, some provision must be made for a minimal level of access.

The case against general taxation as a method of funding transportation is eloquently made by Thomas Hardin in an article titled "Tragedy of the Commons."[41] He describes a pasture open to cattle grazing and available to all farmers at no cost. The farmers enjoy a growth in milk production with the addition of each cow, with no increase in grazing cost. Each farmer continues to add to the herd, enjoying the full utility of the grazing privileges. This practice however begins to detract from the pasture's ability to support all the herds and the milk production from each cow begins to reduce. The farmer's rational decision is to add more cows so that he or she can continue selling the same amount of milk. All farmers join in this practice and the pasture is increasingly less able to support the herd. As Hardin stated it: "Each man is locked into a system that compels him to increase his herd without limit, in a world that is limited each pursuing his own best interest in a society that believes in the freedom of the common." The analogy represents precisely the decision process of the pest control company that must add additional service vehicles to satisfy a set number of customers or the analogy represents each of us who consider it more convenient to drive as single occupants in an automobile. A general tax or a gasoline tax that establishes little or no relationship between use and cost will eventually suffer the "tragedy of the commons."

Regardless of the method of funding used, what is perhaps most disconcerting is that transportation policy is frequently overlooked as a critical concern compared to other public agenda. The short-term perspectives that are the result of the election process and a lack of understanding of the role of transportation in economic development makes transportation funding an agenda that does not attract the politician and leaves a leadership vacuum. A lack of political courage to make difficult decisions in transportation policy leads to a worsening surface transportation condition. Even if funding becomes available years of rebuilding and retrofitting "under traffic" will be very challenging. Unlike new alignment projects typical in the twentieth century, capacity expansion will require significant disruption to existing traffic.

The element of pricing in transportation policy is crucial. It is essential that the choices that an individual makes are affected by price at the same time that sufficient transportation resources are provided. As a country, we are caught in our own desire to have an unlimited supply of transportation facilities at a perceived cost of zero. Without political vision and leadership our economic progress will begin to lag, though not attributable to any particular political group or political leader. The relationship between the economy and mobility for passengers and freight is fundamental to any long term policy and must be supported by funding mechanisms that establish user pricing systems. Further, taxation and transportation investment policies must be considered in the context of other competing economies.

2

o o o o o o o o o o o o o o o o o o o o o o o o o o o o o o o o o o

The policy of being too cautious is the greatest risk of all.

—*Jawaharlal Nehru*

WHAT IS AT RISK?

It is clear from the vast amount of data and research available that a close relationship exists between transportation and economic vitality. Given the overwhelming support for this from research, what are the risks of doing nothing or continuing on the same transportation policy course? What data indicate the need for an expanded supply of surface transportation and in what specific ways should transportation be provided? What if we remain on the current policy course. What are the likely outcomes of such inaction?

The Need for Transportation Facilities

Many studies have been performed that provide incontrovertible evidence that the needs for surface transportation are enormous and growing at an alarming rate. The United States government performs studies annually to determine the transportation needs of the country and a recent compilation of transportation needs by the state departments of transportation is documented in the American Association of State Highway and Transportation Officials (AASHTO) report. This report states that the annual highway funding by all levels of government should be $92 billion, simply to maintain physical condition and performance characteristics over the next 20 years. The current level of funding is $64.5 billion,[42] and represents about two thirds of the calculated need to maintain current conditions. Further, to improve the system over the next twenty years, an investment level of $125.6 billion would be needed annually by all levels of government. This would improve pavement conditions by about 15 percent,

33

particularly in urban areas. If such a level of investment were made over the next twenty years, it is estimated that delay would fall by almost 13 percent despite the expected growth in vehicle miles traveled. It is also projected that average speeds would improve and user costs would be reduced from $937 per 1,000 miles of travel to $913[43]. This equates to roughly a $60 billion-a-year saving, almost equivalent of the total annual expenditures being made today. The cost benefit of such expenditure levels is clear. As we will see later, however, more of the same type of funding is only part of the answer. The AASHTO report places the 2002 total value of needs for highways and bridges at $254 billion. These are the best data available from the state departments of transportation working in cooperation with the federal government.

While this seems like a huge number, it should be considered that this compilation of transportation needs is not static. As travel demand increases, these costs will increase over time. In addition, the effect of inflation will further add to the unfunded needs balance. While it might be difficult to project the impact of future travel demand, a simple analysis of the impact of inflation is startling.

If the AASHTO data is to be accepted, the highway and bridge needs are approximately $254 billion. Applying an arbitrary cost increase index of 5 per cent per year, the existing needs would grow in cost as follows:

Table 8: Inflationary Effect on Transportation Needs

5 years	$324 billion
10 years	$413 billion
15 years	$528 billion
20 years	$673 billion

This means that if nothing were done to correct present deficiencies, it would require approximately 2 1/2 times the funding twenty years from now to correct them. Considering the recent price increases for cement and steel resulting from demand by China, India and other large, fast growing nations, these estimates may be conservative. It is not likely that the competition for building materials will reduce over the next twenty years either. Cost increases are not new phenomena, but they are rarely accounted for in transportation needs analyses.

Importantly, these inflation calculations assume no growth in the base number as a result of increased highway travel. With increased demand for surface transportation, the AASHTO numbers will grow, and at accelerated rates. Considering the growth in passenger and freight traffic over the last twenty-year period, it would be reasonable to believe that this will continue.

While costs have continued to rise and are rarely accounted for in estimates of transportation needs, revenue generated through the surrogate user fee of gasoline tax has been decreasing faster than anticipated.

This divergence of financial projections for revenue and expenditure is further hampered by the unrelenting demand for surface transportation that is the result of pricing policies. These policies are hinged on the use of gasoline tax as the primary method of funding. The genesis of these taxation methods is the beginning of the twentieth century when the surface transportation system of highways was just beginning in the U.S. This invisible connection between the payment of gasoline tax and the use of the highway camouflages the pricing relationship. When a commodity is priced at a perceived level of zero, we should expect unlimited demand and an inability to provide sufficient supply. This compounding effect, when considered in relation to an increasing and non-linear congestion curve, ultimately portends a negative economic effect.

The Cost of Traffic Congestion

What are the costs of not adequately providing for surface transportation? Costs can be generally categorized into congestion/time delay and safety. While these factors relate to one another and affect one another, for demonstration purposes and simplicity they are considered separately.

Traffic congestion costs are a composite of time delay, increased vehicle operating costs, accident repair and increased air pollution. The costs result from the interference that occurs between vehicles in a traffic stream. While these costs increase slowly at first, vehicular flow passes from a smooth, laminar flow to more turbulent stop and go conditions, congestion costs increase quickly. It is generally agreed that this phenomenon occurs on a geometric scale as the capacity of the highway is approached. Traffic increases of 10 per cent have different effects on traffic congestion costs depending on whether the highway is near capacity or at some lower level of usage. Initially, delays and accident risks increase at a slow pace as traffic volumes increase and then increase at a faster rate as each unit of additional traffic comes onto the roadway. Each incident reduces capacity of the roadway and the cycle feeds upon itself, ending in gridlock. This phenomenon is very difficult to generalize into a predictive model and can only be evaluated for each unique setting. However, it is possible to grasp a concept of the rate of growth of congestion through a simple analysis of a theoretical roadway section having typical distributions of traffic throughout a travel day.

Imagine a one-lane roadway with a capacity of 2,250 vehicles per hour, a total theoretical capacity (24 hours per day) of 54,000. This, of course, assumes that the demand for the roadway is 2,250 per hour during each hour of the day and that perfect driving conditions and perfect driver behavior is in place. Actual demand, of course, varies by these factors and the time of day. Traffic in the peak demand periods of the morning and evening hours is heaviest and lightest in the late evening and early morning. Table 9 below shows a hypothetical distribution of travel demand.

Table 9: Existing Conditions of Hypothetical Roadway Delay

EXISTING

Hour	Volume	Vol>Cap.	Cum.	Delay (Min.)
12-1AM	150	-2100		
1-	150	-2100		
2-	150	-2100		
3-	150	-2100		
4-	150	-2100		
5-	150	-2100		
6-	600	-1650		
7-	900	-1350		
8-	1500	-750		
9-	1950	-300		
10-	2100	-150		
11-	1650	-600		
Noon-1	1800	-450		
1-	1650	-600		
2-	1500	-750		
3-	1800	-450		
4-	1950	-300		
5-	1650	-600		
6-	900	-1350		
7-	600	-1650		

Table 9: Existing Conditions of Hypothetical Roadway Delay (Continued)

EXISTING

Hour	*Volume*	*Vol>Cap.*	*Cum.*	*Delay (Min.)*
8-	300	-1950		
9-	300	-1950		
10-	300	-1950		
11-Mid.	300	-1950		
	22650	-31350		0
	Volume	Vol>Cap.		(Min.)

The exactness of this travel demand is not of crucial importance since differences between the available capacity and the demand are carried over to the following hour. Whether the delay occurs at 8 a.m. or 9 a.m. is somewhat irrelevant. The theoretical maximum capacity for each hour remains 2,250 vehicles per hour, the demand or volume of traffic varies and the difference, positive or negative, affects the following hour. If the demand volume exceeds 2,250 in any hour then the roadway is assumed to be over capacity and the excess volume is carried to the next hour. When demand volume drops below 2,250 some of the accumulated excess demand can be accommodated. The delay is calculated by dividing the accumulated excess volume by 37.5, which is the theoretical capacity of the roadway per minute.

In the "existing" condition travel volumes do not exceed the capacity of the roadway at any point during the day. This facility would be operating at free flow conditions.

If this roadway experienced national average growth for a five-year period, delays would increase. The average growth in vehicle miles traveled over the last ten years in the United States has been 2.6 per cent for 2-axle vehicles, 3.7 per cent for single unit trucks and 3.0 per cent for truck combinations.[44] If an average growth were assumed to be 3 per cent each year, the compound growth over five years would be 16 per cent. Table 10 shows the results.

Table 10: Traffic Growth and Delay After 5 Years

Hour	Volume	Increase 16% 5 yr @ 3% Vol>Cap.	Cum.	Delay (Min.)
12-1AM	174	-2076		
1-	174	-2076		
2-	174	-2076		
3-	174	-2076		
4-	174	-2076		
5-	174	-2076		
6-	696	-1554		
7-	1044	-1206		
8-	1740	-510		
9-	2262	12	12	0
10-	2436	186	198	6
11-	1914	-336		
Noon-1	2088	-162		
1-	1914	-336		
2-	1740	-510		
3-	2088	-162		
4-	2262	12		
5-	1914	-336		
6-	1044	-1206		
7-	696	-1554		
8-	348	-1902		
9-	348	-1902		
10-	348	-1902		
11-Mid.	348	-1902		
	26274 Volume	-27726 Vol>Cap.		6 (Min.)

A five-year average growth in traffic in this hypothetical example, which is a compounded 16 per cent, results in two hours of the day in which the hourly capacity of the roadway is exceeded by demand in that hour and no hours in which capacity is exceeded due to carry over of volume and a total delay of 6 minutes for the one lane of traffic. Tables 11,12 and13 contained in the Appendix show similar calculations for 10, 15 and 20-year growth respectively. Table 14 summarizes the results for the hypothetical case from today's free flow conditions to the conditions expected twenty years from now.

Table 14: Hypothetical Effects of Growth on Highway Delay

Years	Growth	Hours Vol>Cap	Accum Vol>Cap	Delay Minutes
Today	0	0	0	0
5	16	2	2	6
10	34	5	10	243
15	56	10	13	936
20	81	10	19	3977

The analysis suggests that an average three percent growth in traffic volume on a roadway will morph from free flow to near gridlock in twenty years. There are many caveats crucial to this conclusion. First, there is no provision for interaction with the surrounding highway network or other modes of transportation. Most highways in America have alternative routes or alternative modes of transportation that can be taken once congestion leads to unacceptable delay.

Secondly, there is no provision for modification in behavior, traveling different times of the day etc. and lastly, it is assumed that no new capacity of any kind will be provided in the corridor. There is also an inherent assumption that economic growth will continue, even if it is nearly impossible to navigate the corridor. Finally, it is assumed that no additional accidents or other roadside incidents occur as a result of traveling close in an increasingly congested environment. This analysis is intended to demonstrate that congestion delay is a non-linear function resulting from linear growth in traffic volumes.

Several observations are appropriate from this hypothetical analysis. In first year or base case, a free flow condition exists. By the fifth year conditions are still near free flow with only 6 minutes of delay. However, at the end of twenty years of linear 3% growth, there are ten hours that are over capacity but nineteen hours that experience delay. The delay that would be theoretically experienced by the driving public would increase from 0 minutes to 3977 minutes in the following progression 0, 6, 243, 936, 3977 while traffic volumes would grow 81% linearly over the twenty year period.

To describe highway capacity and performance traffic engineers use a descriptive categorization termed "level of service." Table 15 below illustrates typical statistics for levels of service A through F.[45]

Table 15: Levels of Service

LOS	Speed Range (mph)	Flow Range (veh/hour/lane)	Density Range (veh/mile)
A	Over 60	Under 700	Under 12
B	57-60	700-1,100	12-20
C	54-57	1,100-1,550	20-30
D	46-54	1,550-1,850	30-42
E	30-46	1,850-2,000	42-67
F	Under 30	Unstable	67-Maximum

The table gives an indication of how speeds reduce and volumes increase as traffic density increases. Level of service A is the free flow condition and as volumes increase level of service decreases until a level of service F is reached and gridlock occurs. If the need for additional capacity or alternatives is not recognized until near gridlock occurs, the delays will grow throughout the network of roadways as vehicles seek other routes and the peak hour stretches throughout the network for a longer period.

Considering that major transportation projects require 10 years or more on average to design and construct, the effect of not providing additional capacity on some regular basis only worsens conditions when funds do become available. If finding is delivered in large bursts rather than smoothly over a long period, the price of ultimately correcting the decline in the level of service is increased. Even if unlimited funding were provided, the design and construction must be accomplished in a way that does not unduly increase construction prices.

A consistent measurement of congestion in the U.S. is being performed by the Texas Transportation Institute. The institute has been collecting data on congestion in 85 major metropolitan areas of the United States from 1982 to the present and has documented a substantial growth in congestion. The TTI report found that urban traffic congestion currently costs the nation $63.2 billion annually in the cost of wasted fuel and lost time.[46] Neither property damages nor fatalities resulting from accidents were included. The cost of congestion has increased from 14.2 billion in 1982.[47]

A specific example of this cost is demonstrated by a study of freight in Florida. Delay introduces significant costs for freight hauling. Independent research conducted for the Florida Transportation Commission documented the cost of delay for a typical tractor-trailer to be $1.00 per minute.[48] The Texas Transportation Institute uses $71.05 per hour for the cost of delay for a heavy vehicle and $13.45 per hour of delay for a passenger car. Since profit margins in freight hauling are relatively small, delay is not financially tolerable. From 1996 through 2001 the average profit margin achieved by major United States carriers was 3.0 per cent. In 2001 it was 1.4 per cent.[49] A few major disruptions in traffic could eliminate already slim profit margins from the highway freight business and result in increased costs for all goods shipped.

The economic impact of traffic congestion is not just about major freight haulers. It affects local distributors of products, as well. Businesses engaged in providing services such as real estate, pest control, air conditioning, pool cleaning, lawn services etc. are affected. This cost is directly related to costs resulting from increased congestion. These costs are absent any provision for increases in service volume. There is a real business and personal cost of traffic congestion.

The Texas Transportation Institute summarizes the congestion issue quite explicitly.[50]

> *While there have been some infrastructure improvements, road capacity in the United States has not kept up with vehicle travel over the past two decades. While traffic delays per person caused by traffic congestion increased considerably from 1982 to 2000—236 percent, and travel and population increased significantly, 72 percent and 19 percent, respectively; there has been little additional road capacity. Since 1982, only 6 percent in new road mileage has been built to accommodate new travel demand.*

Some effects of delay are not quantifiable or at least have not been quantified. For example, what is the value of an assembly line component that does not reach the destination in time to keep the line in continuous operation? What is the value of a proposal that doesn't make the deadline for delivery? It is conceivable that the entire value of the product or service is eliminated as a result of late arrival. Time utility can have a major impact on the value of goods or services.

Quality of life issues are also impacted by congestion delays. There are missed family events, school events, and a myriad of other personal and important occasions that go unaccounted in the cost analyses of delay. While perhaps not quantifiable, the effects on quality of life resulting from congestion and delay are nonetheless real to every citizen and they are considered by industry when contemplating the location for new headquarters, plants, warehouses and other business centers.

Other societal costs are evident through a phenomenon that has come to be known as road rage. In essence, it is an outward display of the dissatisfaction with the service provided by our surface transportation systems. With each moment sitting at a light or moment of delay caused by traffic jams, the sense of urgency heightens and stress grows, sometimes ending in undesirable behavior. Uncertainty of travel time can also contribute to dangerous behavior. It is more acceptable if a trip regularly takes two hours than one that should take 30 minutes requires an hour. Such uncertainty can result in disproportionate economic consequences such as the proposal that doesn't arrive on time or the component that doesn't arrive at the assembly line in time. It can also result in a missed birthday, a child's baseball game or school play. All of these possibilities add to the unsavory and dangerous behavior of road rage.

The Economics of Safety

Another economic facet of inadequate transportation facilities is safety. While it is not possible to fully quantify human suffering associated with the 8,300 injuries that occur on America's highways every day, costs incurred can be calculated. Further, the loss of life is a horrible and personal tragedy and any cost analyses are wholly inadequate. However, fatality statistics are an important factor to be considered when prioritizing projects.

Of the 44,313 transportation fatalities that occurred in 2000, 41,945 were highway related.[51] The transportation deaths related to all other modes, including aviation (commercial and general), railroad (including railroad grade crossings), waterborne (vessel related and recreational boating) and transit were approximately 2,800. Trends in the data also demonstrate the costs of human behavior with alcohol, speed and inadequate protective equipment in motorcycle deaths. The construction of safer highways and vehicles has improved highway safety, in particular the interstate highway system and urban expressways. Safer vehicles with features designed to avoid crashes and minimize impact have found their way into the modern automobile. In the last twenty years, there has been an increased focus on driver behavior as well. More seat belt compliance and a reduction in drunk driving have been a result of tougher laws and greater enforcement and research in the field of human factors generally has intensified. All have contributed to the safer driving environment.

Minimizing fatalities has been a continuous priority in transportation policy and safety programs at all levels of government. Individuals, congress, public agencies and automobile manufacturers have initiated efforts. We have created safer automobiles, safer highways and changed individual behaviors. The fatalities on America's highways have reduced significantly, when measured against vehicle miles traveled. In 1960 there was one fatality for every 19.7 million vehicle miles traveled. By 2000 that statistic had changed to 65.6 million vehicle miles per fatality, a 330 per cent improvement.[52]

A similar trend can be seen in the number of highway accidents and injuries over time. In 1990 there were 6,471,000 highway accidents and 3,230,666 injured people compared to 6,323,000 and 3,032,672 respectively in 2001.[53] If measured against vehicle miles traveled, the improvement would have been even more pronounced. This is wonderful result given the increase in traffic and congestion, especially on urban highways. Naturally as highways become more congested, speeds have reduced and this has also helped in the reduction of fatalities. A measure of safety independent of miles driven or congestion levels is property damage and insurance costs. Figure 3 below shows actual auto insurance expenditures and projections through 2004 by the Insurance Information Institute.

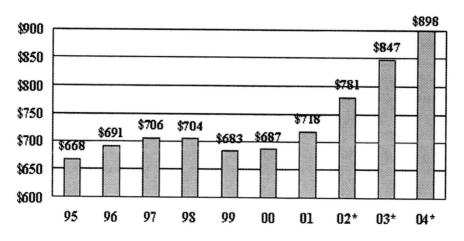

Figure 3: Average Consumer Expenditures on Auto Insurance

The average cost of auto insurance rose by 8.4 per cent in 2002 and was expected to rise another 9 per cent in 2003. The Insurance Information Institute attributes this increase to be the result of a significant increase in claims in the year 2000. Since data is analyzed and rate requests subsequently prepared, there is a lag between historical data on increased claims and premiums.

Another measure of auto insurance cost is the nonstandard insurance industry. Nonstandard insurance is that written for drivers considered to be more at risk of an accident than the general populace. From 1995 to 2001 the percent of private passenger automobile insurance that is nonstandard has risen from 16.2 per cent to 20.4 per cent. The premiums for this market increased 57 per cent in the six-year period.[54]

The National Highway and Traffic Safety Administration estimates the total economic loss of motor vehicle crashes in the United States to be $230.568 billion in 2000. This represents an approximately $80 billion increase (53 per cent) over the 1994 figure of $150.469 billion. The cost of automobile safety is clearly a factor to consider in the economics of transportation.

Gasoline Tax—A Reducing Funding Source

Clearly, the adequacy of our transportation system has an impact upon the economy, but many believe this to be a limited relationship. While a correlation between the two is accepted by most, it is a commonly held view that the economic effects of transportation are long term. We are an adaptable society and optimistically believe technology and new ways of coping with traffic congestion will minimize that impact. However, data would suggest that such thinking is quickly becoming a luxury we can't afford. Several trends are converging to bring transportation policy closer to the need for action and the policy of maintaining the gasoline tax as the primary source of transportation funding is becoming more questionable.

Currently in the U.S. the gasoline tax is the near exclusive source of surface transportation funding for expanding and maintaining transportation facilities in the United States. It is also well known that this primary source of funding will likely decrease over the next decade and beyond. However, there are indications that that this decrease may happen more quickly and this is occurring at the same time that the backlog of transportation needs is building. Decreases in gasoline tax revenue are a result of many factors and some are well known such as improvements in fuel efficiency. However, some are the result of actions taken in other important policy areas such as changes in air quality standards, federal funds allocation processes and further improvements in fuel economy precipitated by advances in automobile technology.

While it may not be immediately clear that the application of air quality standards has a relationship to reduced transportation tax revenues, unintended consequences are a likely outcome. There is no debate that air quality is an enormously important agenda and one that should be pursued aggressively. Great strides have been made since the early 1970's in air quality that would not have been possible without technological improvements that reduced automobile emissions. The technological improvements and the air quality policies that stimulated these improvements are highly laudable.

There is however, a relationship between some air quality policies and future reductions in gasoline tax revenue that are not immediately evident. The relationship of air quality regulatory standards and transportation revenue is multilayered. Vehicle emissions technology has significantly improved urban air quality over the last twenty-five years and further improvements are on the horizon.

Partial Zero Emission Vehicles (PZEV) are now available for only $200-$300 more than standard models and are being sold in California today. Approximately 170,000 will be sold in the United States this year. Additionally, Zero Emission Vehicle (ZEV) technology is available commercially but has experienced less commercial success because of convenience and cost issues. However, it has been argued that electrically operated vehicles (one version of zero emission vehicle) could, depending upon the methods used to generate electrical power, actually lessen air quality. If, for example, the air quality controls on fixed point sources of electrical power generation are inadequate, the air pollution resulting could be greater than the gasoline powered vehicle it replaces. Though much progress has occurred in mobile point sources of emissions (primarily the automobile), standards have continued to tighten.

Air pollutants commonly tracked by environmental protection agencies include carbon monoxide, particulate matter, nitrogen oxides, lead, sulfur dioxide and ground level ozone. Ozone, which is the product of volatile organic compounds and nitrogen oxides, is regularly tracked and has the most potential to affect transportation system revenues in unexpected ways.

Metropolitan areas in the United States that failed to attain air quality standards are designated non-attainment areas. The number of metro areas that failed attain to the air quality standard for ozone of 120 parts per billion (measured as an average of readings over a one-hour period) in 2001 was 30.[55] In July 1997 new air quality standards were promulgated. These standards require that no more than 80 parts per billion of ozone can exist when averaged over an 8-hour period. As of June 23, 2003, the United States Environmental Protection Agency indicated that there were 53 ozone, 11 carbon monoxide, 24 sulfur dioxide, 64 PM-10, and 3 lead non-attainment areas in the United States. There were no NO2 non-attainment areas in the United States.[56] While it is not yet clear how many additional metropolitan areas will fall into non-attainment as a result of the implementation of the new standard, it is estimated by one environmental firm[57] that approximately 525 counties (mostly in the northeast, southwest and great lakes urban counties) will be designated non-attainment for ozone.

While at first glance air quality regulation may seem unrelated to the question of gasoline tax revenue, there may be a direct relationship because of unintended consequences. When an area is determined to be in non-attainment a transportation plan must be put into place to reduce the ozone emanating from "mobile point sources" (i.e., motor vehicles). "Fixed point sources" such as power generation or industrial sources are also addressed by regulation and remediation is through pollution equipment installation and in some cases conversion from coal or petroleum to natural gas. However, a simple and common method of reducing mobile point sources or automobile emissions is the introduction of an oxidizing agent to gasoline blend. Introducing oxidizing agents requires no modifications to vehicles, mixes easily with gasoline and is easily and quickly implemented, thereby meeting the regulatory requirements of a transportation plan.

Initially, methyl tertiary-butyl ether, MTBE was used as the oxidizing agent throughout the United States. However, in 2001, a class action suit was filed involving eighteen states in which it was alleged that MTBE had contaminated water supplies and MTBE has been phased out as an oxidizing agent for automotive fuel.

An alternative oxidizing agent that is produced in quantity and readily available is ethanol, and, it has become the predominant oxidizing agent additive for gasoline. Ethanol is made from corn, a commodity produced in great surplus and one that represents a renewable source of energy. Under current federal law when ethanol is mixed with gasoline, the product (gasohol) enjoys a partial exemption from the federal gasoline tax. A 10 per cent Ethanol and 90 per cent gasoline mix, gasohol receives a 7 cent exemption from the 18 cents per gallon federal gasoline tax. Similar provisions exist for some state gasoline taxes. However, on the federal level approximately 39 per cent of the gasoline tax on gasohol is exempted when ethanol is mixed with gasoline to create gasohol.

The exemption for gasohol has already had a negative impact on gasoline tax revenues and it has been suggested that the exemption should cease. This concern might elevate as the effects of new standards on metropolitan areas occur over the next few years. However, it will be difficult to eliminate this exemption. The politics of such tax break elimination for a renewable energy source might be considered inconsistent with sound energy policy not to mention the congressional politics. Considering the number of corn producing states and the powerful voting block that they represent in Congress, it seems unlikely that this exemption will be completely eliminated and there are economic and social reasons that resonate with many constituencies. To the contrary, using a bio-generated fuel that is favorable to the environment and one that reduces the importation of oil would likely enjoy significant public and political support.

In addition to the effects of tax exemptions for gasohol on transportation revenue, federal gas tax revenues are undergoing further downward adjustments resulting from previous budget provisions. These adjustments are the product of adjustments included in the Transportation Equity Act for the 21st Century, TEA-21 that was passed in 1997. That authorizing legislation attempted to ensure that all revenues received would be spent for transportation rather than building balances in the transportation trust fund. The provision was titled Revenue Aligned Budget Authority or RABA which served to accelerate transportation expenditures and draw down trust fund balances. Provisions were included for reducing the authorization of expenditure if revenues were less than anticipated. The downward adjustment required to comply with the RABA provisions has been calculated at $9 billion. Although there is concern about how the adjustments should be made for previous expenditures, it is nevertheless money previously obligated for expenditure that is not available for new projects.

In addition to these events, the gasoline tax has been used in the past for deficit reduction and other purposes. Table 16 below was reproduced from congressional testimony of the American Association of State Highway and Transportation Officials in 2002.

Table 16: Gasoline Tax Uses 1956-1997

Changes in Gasoline Tax: 1956-Present				
Year	Total Tax	Highway Account	Mass Transit Account	Deficit Reduction	Leaking Undergound Storage Tank
1956	3	3	-	-	
1959	4	4	-	-	
1983	9	8	1	-	
1987	9.1	8	1	-	0.1
1990	14.1	10	1.5	2.5	0.1
1993	18.4	10	1.5	6.8	0.1
1995	18.4	12	2	4.3	0.1

Table 16: Gasoline Tax Uses 1956-1997 (Continued)

1997	18.4	15.44	2.86	-	0.1

Source: FHWA, "Financing Federal Aid Highways," 1999

While there was an increase in the gas tax allocated to highways over the period, revenues from the gasoline tax have not been exclusively used for highways. The data show that from 1990 to 1995 a considerable amount of the gas tax went to general deficit reduction, and, since 1983, an increasing amount has been allocated to other than highways.

There is no question that policy initiatives for modes other than highways are crucial to surface transportation, especially in urban areas. Mass transit and other modes are important components of a multimodal transportation policy. The fact remains however, that an increasing amount of gasoline tax has been allocated to non highway purposes even as the total gasoline tax revenue has been decreasing. Since 1997 there has been no change in the gasoline tax levy. However, since 1997 there has been enormous growth in the use of highways, especially arterial highways, by both passenger and freight vehicles for various reasons, some out of preference and some resulting from the inherent flexibility of the truck and the fundamental changes in business processes.

The Arrival of the Hybrid Vehicle

Changes are also occurring in the basic technological design of the automobile that will affect transportation revenue. Hydrogen-powered vehicles offer great promise in the future and research efforts are underway to develop them but barring major breakthroughs, they will not be commercially viable for ten or more years. The hybrid vehicle, however, is commercially available today and increasing sales will ultimately have a significant impact on gasoline tax revenues.

The hybrid automobile uses a small diesel or gasoline engine to produce electrical energy that is stored and ultimately used to propel the vehicle. These hybrid automobiles are significantly more fuel efficient than even the most efficient gasoline engine. These hybrid vehicles are commercially available today and achieve 50 miles per gallon or about twice that of current Corporate Average Fuel Economy, CAFE standards for the passenger vehicle fleet. CAFÉ standards were introduced to stimulate greater fleet fuel efficiency from the major automakers in the U.S.

Hybrid vehicles have been commercially available since December 1999 with the introduction of the Honda Insight and in June 2000 by the Toyota Prius, and the pace of sales is quickening. Sport utility vehicles, SUVs are beginning to be manufactured as hybrids as well. Figure 4 shows the launch dates for various hybrid vehicles and increasingly include SUVs. The expansion of hybrid vehicles will likely further erode the gasoline tax revenue generated on a per mile basis. It is estimated that the annual sales of hybrid autos in the United States will reach 500,000 by 2007. While still a small portion of the 16,000,00 sold, the numbers of hybrids are growing quickly.

Hybrids Launch Dates in North Amreica

Make and model	Release date
Honda Insight hatchback	December 1999
Toyota Prius sedan	June 2000
Honda Civic hybrid sedan	April 2002
Ford Escape SUV	December 2003
GMC Sierra pickup	2004
Chevy Silverado pickup	2004
Lexus RX 330 SUV	2005
Saturn VUE SUV	2005
Chevrolet Equinox SUV	2006
Chevrolet Malibu sedan	2007

Figure 4: Commercial Launch Dates for Hybrids in North America

Hybrid vehicle sales are driven by their reduced emissions and greater fuel efficiency. Hybrids important in helping automobile manufacturers meet regulatory requirements for efficiency. Improvements in fuel efficiency have been developing since 1975 with introduction of CAFE standards. CAFE standards were intended to regulate improvements in the fuel efficiency of the fleet and to reverse the trend to more powerful vehicles. By the time CAFE standards were introduced in 1974, average fuel efficiency of the fleet had fallen to 12.9 miles per gallon (mpg). CAFÉ standards mandated 18 mpg in 1978 models, which rose to 27.5 by 1985. While there was a reduction to 26 mpg for a short period, the standards were returned to 27.5 in 1990 and have remained at that level since. Such mandated changes in vehicle efficiency have reduced the gasoline tax per mile driven by more than half and while important for many reasons, the effectiveness of gasoline tax as a reasonable surrogate "user fee" for highway use has been reduced.

While all of these changes have occurred, the SUV has grown in prominence. The entire growth in 2-axle 4-tire vehicles from 1990 to present is composed of vans and sport utility vehicles. The CAFE standard for sport utility vehicles is currently 20.7 mpg. Interestingly, most SUVs and pickups, and all vans, were permitted to emit 29 per cent to 47 per cent more carbon monoxide and 75 per cent to 175 per cent more nitrogen oxides than passenger cars. The standards were made consistent with passenger cars only in the last two years. Air quality standards for SUVs and vans, equivalent to automobiles, began with 2003 models for lighter vehicles but larger SUVs (over 6000 pounds) are also exempt. These larger vehicles also enjoy accelerated depreciation for business purposes which encourages businesses to purchase such vehicles. These tax provisions were originally intended to assist agricultural businesses but since been utilized by many that do not require such a large vehicle for urban business purposes.

Accelerating Congestion

It has been demonstrated earlier that traffic congestion growth is a non-linear function and data from the Texas Transportation Institute corroborates that conclusion. The institute has documented that from 1982 to 2002 population has increased 19 per cent, travel increased 71 per cent and congestion 236 per cent. This has occurred even though more trips were taken on bus, commuter rail and light rail over this same period. While significant growth occurred in the volume of transit trips, the rate of growth of vehicle miles traveled by automobiles, sport utility vehicles and vans continued.

The transportation Institute data clearly show that "rush-hour" trips are taking longer and the length of the "rush-hour" is consistently growing. This is consistent with the theoretical congestion example presented. Not only is congestion increasing on specific highway segments but the number of miles of highway experiencing highway congestion has increased. Perhaps the most appropriate expression of congestion is the total delay that occurs on the entire roadway network over time. As congestion increases on arterial routes, it should be expected than other routes will experience increases in congestion until ultimately the entire network becomes congested.

The effect of network congestion is reflected in the mobility data produced by the Texas Transportation Institute and reveals a disconcerting conclusion. In the graph below are shown the vehicle miles of travel (VMT) from 1982 to 2002 and total hours of delay for the 75 urban areas included in the study. From 1982 to 2000 the VMT in the 75 urban areas doubled. However, the total hours of delay increased five fold, and the cost of congestion increased eight fold. As VMT doubled, annual delay went from 742 million hours to 3.6 billion and the cost of congestion from $8.2 billion to $69.5 billion.[58] It seems clear that the accumulated hours of delay and cost of congestion increase at a much faster rate than the freeway VMT. Over the eighteen years delay has grown at a rate two and one-half times greater than freeway vehicle miles traveled, and congestion costs at a rate four times faster than freeway vehicle miles traveled. If the hypothetical case for congestion presented earlier is indicative, the congestion delay and cost curves should be expected to grow at an even steeper rate in the future.

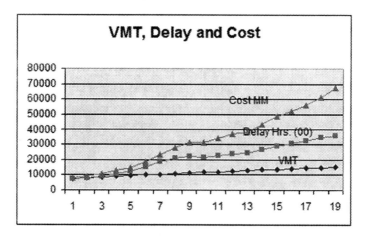

Figure 5: Urban Mobility Study: Freeway DVMT(000), Delay hours (00)
and Congestion Cost (millions) for 75 Urban Areas

The U.S. has now reached the point that the annual cost of congestion for the 75 urban areas only ($67.4 billion) now exceeds the total highway capital outlay by all levels of government in the entire United States ($64.6 billion).[59] The AASHTO Bottom Line Report indicates a need for $92 billion capital outlay per year to maintain current conditions and $125.6 billion per year to improve conditions. Unless major changes in transportation funding and highway capacity delivery and pricing are implemented, further deterioration seems inevitable.

If steady state funding is assumed for all levels of government and population, vehicle registration and vehicle miles traveled continue to increase at rates that have been consistent since 1960, projections of delay and congestion cost can be made. Likely the rate of increase for delay and congestion costs in the future will be greater than that experienced over the last twenty years. However, if the same rate of growth of VMT continues to 2020, VMT will double; the delay hours for the 75 urban areas would increase from 3.6 billion hours to 18 billion hours, and the cost of congestion would increase from $67 billion to a staggering $536 billion. These delay and cost figures represent only the 75 urban areas selected by the Texas Transportation Institute and represent approximately 64 per cent of the U.S. urban population. To determine the figure for the total congestion cost in the United States, all other urban areas and all rural areas would have to be added. As the highway networks become further saturated with vehicles, delays will expand, accidents will increase and the spiral toward gridlock will continue.

An inspection of the urban mobility data shows a relatively steady growth in delay from 1982 to 2000. If these rates of delay do increase, then the curve representing total delay and the associated costs would be on a steeper slope. This is consistent with our experience as customers of highways. Each occurrence of delay seems to stimulate additional delay and heighten the possibility of incidents. Whether congestion is accelerating or not, the enormity of the issue is glaring and extends beyond the 75 urban areas in the study. Rural areas not reported in the study include vast mileage of the interstate system that has experienced large growth in long-haul truck freight and many smaller cities that have experienced growth in traffic but little additional capacity additions.

The Time for Action

Many believe the underinvestment in transportation capacity to be a long-term policy issue. However, the data demonstrate that a time for action is upon us.

Small variations in assumptions about construction costs and the rate of congestion growth can have a large impact on projections twenty years from now.

The transportation system is already congested to the point that cost of congestion equals the total capital outlay of all levels of government for highways and bridges. If trends continue and actions are not initiated, the cost of congestion will multiply by a factor of eight, to a total of $536 billion, by 2020, assuming that the rate of growth of congestion will remain at present levels. As previously shown, existing needs for highway capital outlay would double in twenty years if inflation is five percent per year. If the rate of inflation is 7 per cent, it takes only ten years.

Highway truck traffic has grown tremendously. Just-in-time inventory, NAFTA and deregulation have all contributed to this growth. These factors are not static. It is estimated that only 28 per cent of today's manufacturing and retailing is performed on a just-in-time basis[60] and as manufacturing, retailing and other segments of the economy strive to compete, they will turn to just-in-time techniques to lessen the costs of operation and in turn increase the necessity for precision in the delivery system.

This chapter has included data on automobile use and has presented evidence of a continuation of growth in vehicle miles traveled, more licensed drivers and more two axle vehicles (though most are vans and SUVs classified as light-duty trucks). Since 1960 there have been continuing trends of urbanization, suburbanization, two-wage-earner families, single-occupant vehicles, and the result has been significant growth in vehicle miles traveled.

It has been demonstrated that gasoline tax revenues will not increase and in fact, are likely to decrease. Gasoline taxes on a per-mile basis will decrease as a result of improvements in fleet fuel efficiency from the commercial introduction of hybrid vehicles, and ultimately, hydrogen or other non-petroleum-based engines. More urban areas will use gasohol as an oxidizing agent in non-attainment areas to meet higher standards for air quality which result in greater gasoline tax exemptions. These factors combined will likely produce reductions in gasoline tax revenue more quickly than has been predicted. If the dependence on gasoline tax for transportation capacity persists, the outlook for congestion relief is dismal.

Any one of these trends would be disconcerting. The probability that they are converging however, leaves the United States at a crisis point. This is significant enough by itself but when viewed in the context of global economic competition, the concerns are heightened. Global competitors are taking actions to build transportation capacity.

Trading alliances, such as the European Union and individual countries, such as China, are planning for economic growth through the provision of transportation. They are building a sound economic foundation by expanding transportation and while doing so they are using pricing systems to affect road user behavior.

The Growing Global Competition

The United States has enjoyed enormous economic growth and prosperity predominantly because of the investment in superior transportation systems. This has occurred for such an enduring period that a malaise has developed about the ability of others to compete economically.

Europe has seen the culmination of a near century old dream in the formation of the European Union. In 2004, ten Eastern European countries became new members of the European Union bringing the total to twenty five. These countries offer natural resources, manpower and new markets that will blend with the economic power and technological capabilities of the existing E.U. countries to create enormous growth potential. Before May, 2004 the E.U. comprised 15 countries, representing a land area of 3.2 million sq.km., a GDP of $9.5 trillion, and a population of 380 million. The ten new countries have added land area of 738,000 sq.km., GDP of $842 billion and 75 million people.[61] More than existing economic power the new entrants to the E.U. have added the potential for economic growth.

Asia, too, is poised as a huge economic trading block; the driving force being China. Recent agreements between China and other countries portend the creation of a huge trading block that is growing quickly. China has seen GDP advances of 8 per cent to 10 per cent annually and is fast converting an agrarian society into an industrial and manufacturing giant. China's plan for economic growth is based upon three emphasis areas: energy production, transportation and education. The transportation component is on a par with the interstate highway system of the United States that will connect the major urban areas and trade centers with highways designed and built to interstate standards. China is also a large trading partner of the United States and is moving aggressively to encourage business.

The European Union and China have plans for transportation and they are being implemented now. These actions and our lack of action could erode our global competitive economic position.

3

"The new electronic interdependence recreates the world in the image of a global village."

—*Marshall McLuhan, "Gutenberg Galaxy," 1962*

THE GLOBAL COMPETITION

Transportation and telecommunications have caused a virtual shrinking of the globe. It is cheaper to ship scrap metal across the Pacific, refine it there and return it than it is to process the same scrap metal in the United States. We are part of a global marketplace and must compete globally. To stay competitive, an underlying superlative transportation system is crucial, since it is the transportation system that creates additional value for products and services because of time and place utility. While we currently possess a transportation system second to none, many of our global competitors are laying technically sound and financially viable plans for vastly improved transportation networks. In contrast, plans for the transportation network of the United States are limited to the funds available and represent a continuation of the incremental allocation of shrinking resources, while the backlog of needs continue to grow. The policy mind set of the United States seems to be based on the assumption that all of the highway capacity needed is in place and our goal now is to maintain that system. Such a policy will not stimulate economic growth.

The future of global competition is trading blocks. These trading blocks are partially formed with the signature of free trade agreements between participating countries. The North America Free Trade Agreement, NAFTA, has established a trading block for the United States, Canada and Mexico and actions are being taken to bring more Latin American and South American countries into the free trade agreement. The competition is currently the European Union and the Asian community, whose largest potential partner is China. Other or expanded trading blocks that will include large developing countries such as India are likely in the future. India too has embarked on the construction of an enormously ambitious transportation system as a part of their economic development plan.

The European Union

Until May, 2004 the European Union was composed of fifteen Western European countries: Austria, Belgium, Denmark, Finland, France, Germany, Greece, Ireland, Italy, Luxemburg, Netherlands, Portugal, Spain, Sweden, and the United Kingdom. Ten Eastern European countries joined in May 2004. Those countries are: Cyprus, the Czech Republic, Estonia, Hungary, Latvia, Lithuania, Malta, Poland, Slovakia and Slovenia. To plan a sound transportation foundation for the European Union, a European Commission white paper was prepared, titled "European Transport Policy for 2010—Time to Decide[62]." The document identifies conditions and issues similar to those in the United States, such as: increased demand for transport services, increased congestion, the economic importance of transportation, safety challenges and potential damage to the environment. The specific proposals in the document include shifting the balance between modes of transport, eliminating bottlenecks, placing users at the heart of transport policy and managing the globalization of transport. In essence the countries of the European Union are planning to use pricing mechanisms to shift behavior away from the automobile and the lorry (truck) to rail and water. The E.U. plans include provisions to generate the necessary revenue to fund surface transportation improvements which include the transportation efficient systems of rail and seaports.

Europe is already a leader in pricing transportation. Since the 1950s an arterial system of highways similar to the interstate system in the U.S. has been funded through a system of concessions. These concessions are equity companies, just as any corporation in the United States. In some cases, the majority ownership is the respective government and in others the government is the minority shareholder. Some wholly owned private concessions also exist. Concessions are granted for a specific period of time, usually thirty years. In that time the concession must recover its original investment of capital and any profit. Pricing is determined either through contract provisions or through negotiations with the government.

These public-private pricing arrangements have been used to construct highway projects, other modal transportation projects and other public works. Concessions have provided a mechanism to self generate the revenues necessary to construct new transportation capacity. Additionally, because transportation and particularly highways are priced, driving behavior and route selection is affected. Recent pricing projects have been implemented in Europe with the predominant purpose of affecting congestion rather than generating revenue. This technique has been used on the London congestion pricing project. The pricing technique places a value on traveling to the city center of London during peak travel hours, originally five pounds and now seven. The implementation of this "price" has reduced congestion in London by about ¼ and the revenues are being used predominantly to fund alternative public transportation systems such as the bus system. Pricing transportation in Europe has therefore been applied for the dual purpose of providing new transportation capacity and affecting demand for transportation.

While the United States has been fortunate to have tax-exempt debt available for toll projects, the experience of the Europeans in equity funding and public-private arrangements may prove to be of enormous value as the United States expands the use of direct user fees. Potentially large amounts of capital can be made available without the requirement for a public referendum or general taxation. Additionally, privately operated entities may tend more toward efficiency than would otherwise be the case.

Two European countries that have not used direct user fees in the past are Austria and Germany. In addition to significant gasoline taxes, Austria has used a taxing mechanism of annual stickers, placed on the vehicle to identify that an annual fee has been paid. Germany has depended exclusively upon gasoline taxes, and other general taxing mechanisms for transportation funding. Historically neither country has used a direct user fee approach. This is changing for both countries. When viewing a map of Europe it becomes apparent that Germany and Austria separate Western Europe from its new Eastern European partners in the E.U.

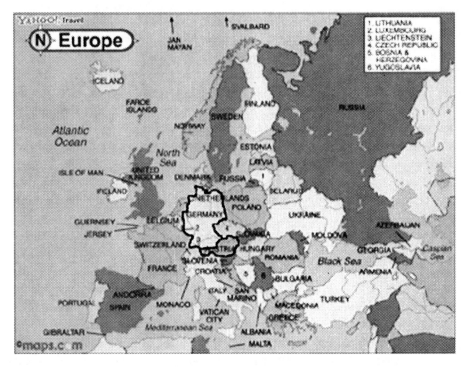

Illustration 2: European Union: West and East separated by Germany and Austria

As such, both have realized significant increases in freight truck traffic and commensurate wear and tear on their highway systems. The existing methods of taxation, particularly fuel taxes, fail to directly charge for highway use. The taxation for these countries can be avoided by purchasing fuel in neighboring countries before entering, or after leaving. Accordingly, maintenance needs have increased in both countries commensurate with growth in traffic (especially truck traffic) and funds are insufficient to maintain the highway systems. Recently, Austria and Germany have undertaken new initiatives to collect tolls for commercial vehicles, trucks over 3 tons. Though the technological approach applied is quite different, the business case is the same. By applying a direct user fee concept both countries are collecting the revenue necessary to maintain their highway systems and secondarily demand is regulated to sustainable levels. The technologies applied for the collection of these new user charges are a significant development in their own right and worthy of consideration. Recent technology advances in the field of electronic toll collection have catalyzed the recent interest in tolling as a funding mechanism for highway capacity.

Austria has begun the installation of nearly 700 overhead gantries or tolling points on the major trade routes for vehicles in excess of 3.5 tons. This method is very similar to electronic toll collection in other parts of the world but with the prime distinction that there is no requirement for the vehicle to stop to pay the toll on the entire network. While other facilities exist that are electronic toll collection only, the Austrian application is the first to be applied on an entire network of roads. Notably the Melbourne Citylink project, the Canadian 407, projects in Santiago, Chile and other projects have similar capabilities but for single projects.

The Austrian radio frequency identification (RFID) system is totally electronic and became operational January 2004. The estimated cost of this new electronic toll collection system is $750 million and will be recovered in the first year of operation. The organization, ASFINAQ, was been assigned responsibility for construction and operation of this system is a functional arm of the Austrian government. Although ASFINAQ operates as an equity corporation, it is owned by the government.

Germany has taken a quite different and unique approach to levying tolls for heavy vehicles. The approach utilizes Global Positioning Satellite and GSM telephony to collect tolls. This approach requires relatively expensive On Board Units, OBU on each truck, costing nearly $1,000 including installation. There are however fewer gantries for toll compliance verification and less capital costs for roadside electronic infrastructure. While Germany has not historically used tolling, starting in January 2005 it implemented a toll for trucks only, on 12,000 kilometers of roadway. Scheduled for implementation in January 2004, the system was delayed until 2005 for technical improvements and to allow sufficient time for truck operators to have the OBUs installed. This was particularly important for operators outside of Germany. It was considered disadvantageous to those outside of Germany to implement on a short schedule, and it was believed that it could restrain trade within the European Union until all heavy vehicles had an opportunity to have OBUs installed. Approximately 1.4 million trucks are required to pay the tolls, and 350,000 are registered outside of Germany. A diagram of how the Toll Collect system will operate is shown in Illustration 3 below.

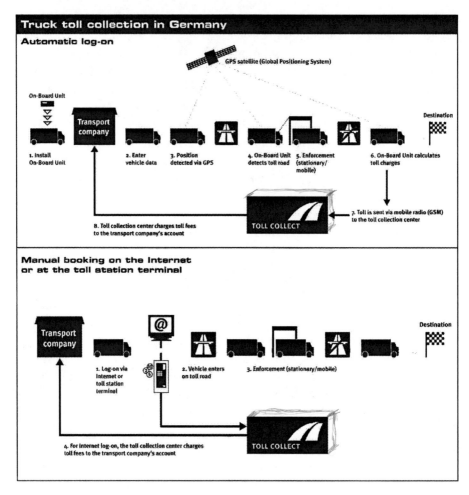

Illustration 3: Diagram of TollCollect GPS toll collection process

In essence heavy vehicles can have the OBU installed and tolls will be collected as the vehicle travels across the 12,000 kilometer arterial system. If the OBU has not yet been installed the alternative is to purchase a trip ticket for a specific route that the vehicle will be traveling. Various toll enforcement locations have been set up to check the vehicle for the validity of the trip tickets and to check any OBU that are not functioning correctly. If the OBU is operating properly the vehicle is not required to stop.

Initially only trucks over 12 tons are required to pay the toll and the charge depends on the vehicle's number of axles, its emission class and the type of vehicle. Conceivably such charges might later be extended down to trucks less than 3.5 tons and will also vary depending on emissions class. This charging methodology is consistent with positions taken by the European Commission. In 2002 the European Commission issued proposed directives on tolling technology that were similar to the GPS methods of TollCollect. These directives were subsequently revised to include both GPS and RFID but a strong case has been made for GPS as the accepted method of pricing truck highway use in the future.

Variations in Electronic Toll Technology.

While GPS could also be used for smaller, personal vehicles; tracking the location of personal vehicles is much different from tracking a commercial vehicle. The location of a commercial vehicle is important logistical information and can have an effect on the profitability of a fleet operation. Knowing the location of an automobile, however, is viewed by many as an imposition on individual privacy. Any scheme that tracks an individual's location will likely be adamantly opposed in most democratic societies where personal privacy is protected.

GPS technology is attractive to the trucking industry, where efficiency is crucial to staying competitive, especially in a just-in-time delivery system where location data could provide a competitive edge. While radio frequency technology could also be used, the choice of one technology is not necessarily mutually exclusive of the other. These two technologies may complement one another depending upon the application.

GPS technology offers several advantages to the toll collector and to truck owners. Knowing the location of a commercial vehicle can be of great value but GPS can also be advantageous to toll operators by reducing the number of points necessary to collect information and therefore avoid some of the cost of toll infrastructure. In a sense, a larger proportion of the technology is embedded in the vehicle OBU and less on the roadside.

One of the more difficult challenges for toll operators using radio frequency technology has been, ensuring the collection of tolls. The predominant method of doing so has been video recordation of vehicle license plates. The systems are typically termed violation enforcement systems. The process works relatively well for automobiles and other single unit vehicles. However, violation enforcement is particularly difficult for tractor-trailer combinations. License plate technology is inherently based on the ability to capture the image of the rear license plate for automobiles. In some systems front and rear license plate images are taken since some states require front and rear licenses. The majority of states however require a rear license plate only. While sufficient for violation enforcement for automobiles, a rear license plate process is inadequate for tractor trailer combinations. While the tractor is owned by the fleet or independent operator, trailers are typically owned by third parties and may be leased or subleased several times over, making it difficult to locate the registered owner of the tractor and therefore the violator.

Secondly, tractor-trailers commonly travel from one state to another or one country to another. Such interstate travel is less common for automobiles. Tracking vehicles through motor vehicle records is also less cumbersome for automobiles because the vehicle is more likely to be registered in the state in which the violation occurred, and there is only one owner of the vehicle. The exception is rented or leased vehicles. Trucks traveling the interstate system are much less likely to be in the state of registration at the time of a toll violation.

The toll collection and violation enforcement process for larger vehicles is particularly important since toll rates for tractor-trailer combinations are usually several times the toll rates charged to automobiles. A large vehicle traveling the entire length of a state will likely have several toll transactions in one trip and could total fifty dollars or more. Unlike a fifty cent toll, a fifty dollar toll is a greater motivation to violate. GPS reduces this toll violation challenge on long haul transactions. GPS technology repeatedly records the location of a vehicle and the toll is computed based upon its location over time and not whether it passed through a particular gantry.

GPS technology seems most appropriate for truck and freight hauling operations while radio frequency technology seems most appropriate for smaller single unit delivery vehicles and automobiles. While the cost of the OBU is larger for the truck, there are benefits that accrue to the owner. The smaller and less costly OBUs are most appropriate for local and regional travel that is more common to the automobile.

A toll technology solution that incorporates both GPS and RFID could be applied in the United States. While the European Union states are tasked with tolling travel between countries within the union, the United States has similar issues but between states. The GPS system could be deployed for trucks and other interstate travel vehicles while the RFID, that is common in most state deployments of ETC, would be used for travelers within the state. The one exception is the Interagency Group in the northeastern U.S. This group represents some 22 toll operators in the northeast and exchanges transactions based on RFID. It is conceivable that interstate travel for automobiles could be handled through an expansion of this concept.

GPS also offers toll operators the opportunity to separate heavier vehicles from automobile traffic. Not only is it more fuel efficient for heavier vehicles to remain moving at toll plazas, separating vehicles with greatly different acceleration and deceleration characteristics minimizes the incidence and severity of accidents and delays. Vehicles are in a slowing and maneuvering process when approaching and leaving a toll plaza. To the extent that the larger and slower vehicles can be separated from the automobile, toll plaza safety is improved.

If a national GPS system were available in the U.S., a national registry might be established and interfaced with local or regional systems. In the case of the European Union a multi-national registry would be needed to provide the same interoperability.

From a policy perspective such an arrangement seems appropriate as well. Interstate freight movement is an economic concern for the whole country born out of improved freight efficiency and the same is true for the European Union. Security in freight movement is also a national concern and could only be assisted by a national registry. Certainly, the issue of freight security extends beyond regional borders and is a major consideration of any proposals in this area.

Considerable investment in dedicated short-range communications (DSRC) technology has occurred regionally in both the United States and the European Union. The investment that has been made over the last fifteen years in RFID toll collection technology need not be lost by the introduction of GPS toll collection approaches. The technologies can be complementary and serve both the regional automobile and long haul truck markets.

E.U. Transportation Plans

These examples of how electronic toll technology are being coordinated in the E.U. and the establishment of implementation policies are indicative of the coordination on transportation policy overall. The E.U. white paper[63] on transportation attempts to bring transportation policy for the E.U. into focus. It clearly identifies the relationship between the economy and transportation and articulates a plan that is presented for discussion, modification and eventual adoption. It is a plan that the European Union countries clearly intend to implement.

The European Union plan documents conditions similar to those of the United States: growing congestion in urban areas and increases in highway freight as opposed to other modes. The E.U. countries have recognized the environmental effects of such events and have prescribed sixty measures centered on charging directly for road use, thereby stimulating use of alternative modes of transportation, and simultaneously targeting investment in the Trans-European network. Europe already prices roadway transportation at a much higher level than the United States and in a manner that is more evident to those using the roadways. While the interstate system provides much of the arterial highway capacity in the U.S., Europe is linked via an arterial system that is largely a network of toll roads. Austria and Germany have been two of the exceptions until the recent implementation of truck tolling. As such, the per mile cost of highway use for an automobile in the United States, based on gasoline tax rates, is about 2 cents per mile, while the tolled networks of Europe are closer to 12 cents per mile in Europe. Further, gasoline taxes and other highway related taxes imposed in Europe are significantly higher than those in place in the U.S.

Consistent with the European Union white paper, rail alternatives to the roadway are being planned and major rail system upgrades are underway. These networks, when completed, will tie the urban centers of Europe together with high-speed rail operations. It is anticipated that such capabilities will allow air travel to better absorb predicted growth over the next twenty years and that some long distance passenger travel will be diverted from the roadway system.

Freight traffic patterns have been systematically analyzed, and the transportation modes that have the greatest efficiency will be encouraged to grow. For example, greater use of ocean-going transport is planned, followed by rail and, finally, motor freight. Preferences for these freight modal choices will be encouraged through the construction of more and improved freight intermodal centers at major ports. Rail freight handling capabilities are being encouraged through the construction of more efficient switching yards and tracking mechanisms. Prices for motorway freight movement will continue to encourage efficient use of the roadway network. A greater spotlight is being placed on the movement of goods from one mode to another, and public funds are being spent to ensure greater efficiency at transfer points. These improvements and others are underway and are being funded and coordinated according to a common plan for transportation.

It is certainly true that Europe and the United States are quite different from one another in political landscape, geography, culture and economic logistics. However, it is also true that Europe has a vision and a method in place for modifying the strategies necessary to ensure that efficient transportation systems will be in place in the long term. In contrast, America seems intent on incremental decision-making heavily influenced by powerful lobbying groups and a prevailing public perception that surface transportation should be free.

China

On the other side of the world is China, with its 1.4 billion people and a desire to be economically progressive. China has been aggressively pursuing economic progress since the end of the cultural revolution and the death of Mao Tse Tung in 1978. As a communist state, China has centralized plans which are enormous in scope and difficult to comprehend how they will be accomplished. Nevertheless, China is moving forward at a frantic pace and will be a significant global economic competitor. China will influence growth in the United States as its trade relationships expand and China competes for markets and the resources necessary to fuel the expanding economy.

China growth rate has been phenomenal. China's economy quadrupled in the last twenty five years, and even if growth slows to 6 per cent, its economy will quadruple again in the next twenty five years. In the same twenty-five-year period, the United States economy doubled. While the U.S. economy is still the largest at about $10 trillion, China is next largest with $6 trillion. Observers of China describe a swift movement from state production to privately owned plant facilities. A recent Washington Post article says that ten years ago most of China's production was from state owned facilities, and now 80 per cent is from private or semi-private companies.[64] While current Chinese transportation systems are substandard to the transportation facilities of the European Union and the United States, progress in constructing transportation infrastructure has been considerable and continues at a rapid pace.

Plans include the construction of 30,000 kilometers of toll roads, vast improvements in air and rail transportation and capitalizing on the advantages offered by the enormous port capacities of Shanghai and Hong Kong. Plans for the future include vast improvements in education, energy, and transportation and are documented in China's tenth Five-Year Plan.[65] In the next five years, China is planning to spend $42.3 billion on subways and light rail systems in twenty cities and will use $32.6 billion to build 850 kilometers of new rail infrastructure; the balance of the $42.3 billion will be invested in rail cars, locomotives and equipment. Most of these improvements are being financed through joint ventures with companies from other parts of the world. As a part of the new five-year plan, China's plans anticipate opening their transport operations market to foreign companies, as well as domestic.

The plan further states that one hundred forty deep-water berths will be built within five years, including 50 container berths, three oil terminals and three ore terminals. Dozens of airports will be built or renovated including; international-standard aviation hubs in Beijing, Shanghai and Guangzhou, 13 large airports, three standby airports and 40 lateral airports.

Transportation plays a large role in the economic plans for China. This has not been the case however for most of the period of communist rule which began in 1949. Inadequate transportation slowed the movement of coal, the movement of agricultural products to markets and delayed the growth of imports and exports. Consequently, the transportation system was underdeveloped and the pace of economic development was constrained. The 1980s were the beginning of transportation system improvements throughout the country and these improvements have remained a priority.

By 1986, China had made substantial progress in its transportation system. The system includes long-distance railroad hauling and long-distance hauling on waterways. Medium-distance rural transportation was predominantly by trucks and buses on national and provincial highways. Water transportation dominated freight movement along the Yangtze River and its tributaries and also in Guangdong Province and the Guangxi-Zhuang Autonomous Region accessed by the Pearl River. All provinces and autonomous regions (with the exception of Tibet) were linked by railroads. Many double tracks, electrified routes, special rail spurs and bridges were added to the system. Subways operated in Beijing and construction was planned for other major cities. National highways were constructed that linked the major provincial capitals to one another and to Beijing and major ports. Roads of various types were built between many towns, but particularly between towns and railroad connections. During this time the merchant marine fleet extended its ports of call throughout the world, but the port facilities in China continued to be an issue until recent improvements and the addition of Hong Kong. During the 1980s airports were substantially improved for both domestic and international travel.

By 1985 the transportation system was capable of handling 2.7 billion tons of goods; rail handled 1.3 billion tons, highways 762 million tons, inland waterways 434 million tons, marine shipping 65 million tons, and airlines handled 195,000 tons. Passenger traffic in 1985 was 428 billion passenger-kilometers; rail accounted for 241.6 billion passenger-kilometers, waterways 17.4 passenger-kilometers, roadways carried 157.3 billion passenger-kilometers, and air traffic was 11.7 billion passenger-kilometers[66].

Ownership of the various transportation modes varied depending upon the perceived importance to the national economy. The railroads were a national asset managed by the Ministry of Railways, but in 1986, contract management of the railways was introduced. Subsequently, five-year contracts between the Railway Ministry and individual railroad bureaus were executed assigning profit and loss responsibility. A state owned company, the China Ocean Shipping Company, operated the merchant fleet, and General Administration of Civil Aviation operated the national airline. Regional airlines were relegated to provincial and municipal control, and the Ministry of Communications administered highways, inland waterways and trucking.

The Seventh Five-Year Plan, which was for the period 1986-1990, placed transportation as a top priority. Thirty-nine of the 190 top priority projects were transportation-related; many of these projects were carried over from 1985. The plan set a priority to increase the cargo carrying capacity of the transportation system by 30 percent in five years. Under the plan, each transportation mode would have to increase its volume by 5.4 percent annually during the five-year period. Included in the plan was a requirement to update passenger and freight transportation for all modes. To do this, the plan outlined an increase in state and local investments but also the use of private funds.

This Seventh Five-Year Plan gave priority to improving the rail lines, particularly those for lines transporting coal or serving major ports. To accomplish this, the plan called for 3,600 kilometers of new rail lines, double tracking 3,300 kilometers of existing railway, and electrifying an additional 4,000 kilometers of railway. Another priority outlined by the plan was for port construction to be increased by 200 million tons, twice the growth prescribed in the previous five-year plan. Highways were also given a high priority in the plan. The plan outlined building new highways and rebuilding 140.000 kilometers of existing highways, increasing the total number by 60,000 kilometers, and bringing the total to one million kilometers.

Today China's GDP is $7.62 trillion and grew 9.1% in 2004[67]. China's transportation system that supports this growth has expanded to 70,058 km of rail line with 22,640 km being dual tracked. The highway system now includes 395,410 km of paved roadways of which 25,130 are expressways. There are 20 deep water ports many of which have experienced significant expansions. There are 169 airports with runways over 2500 meters in length and another 141 with runway between 1500 and 2500 meters[68].

The efficiency with which these transportation improvements have been carried out are second to none. However, it is important to remember that it has also been performed in a state system of government that offers little opportunity for input and that has no property rights to consider. Further, environmental provisions are applied only to the extent that the central government considers it necessary.

A few data points offer insight to China's economic future. While China ranks 148 out of 192 nations in GNP per capita,[69] growth has been at or near 10 per cent annually in the late 1980s and throughout the 1990s. China will host the Olympics in 2008 in Beijing. The first leg of a high speed rail system (a magnetic levitation train) that was to support the Olympics is in service and runs from Shanghai airport to downtown Shanghai. While test tracks for Maglev exist in several countries, this represents the first commercial operation of a Maglev system in the world. China also is hosting the 2010 World Exposition in Shanghai. Construction is underway for a Disney theme park on a man-made island near Hong Kong, and Universal Studios has considered a Universal theme park in Shanghai. Some theme park planners believe that China will rival the United States as an international theme park destination within twenty years.

China has a huge built-in market for its products and services as the cost of living rises (per capita GDP stands at $5600 in 2004). It has resources for petroleum and natural gas rivaling the reserves in the Middle East and it has a plan of action. The political system allows little input into the process and environmental regulations are virtually nonexistent. Although one may question whether China has the most humane method of building a strong economy, the result is revealing of an efficient system.

Through joint ventures between China and private companies, mostly funded by the Chinese government, financial and professional resources have been engaged to build major transportation projects. No less than seven bridges and tunnels traversing over and under the Pearl River in Shanghai have been built in the last decade, and more are under construction. Shanghai business centers, which resemble Manhattan's skyline, stand where open fields stood a decade before and vehicular traffic resembles that of any large metropolitan area.

Illustration 4: Bridge traffic across the Pearl river in Shanghai

In the major business centers of Guangzhou, Shenzhen, Shanghai and Beijing major four-lane divided highways have been built. In the Shenzhen area, high-capacity highways and rail lines have been completed between Hong Kong and Shenzhen and continue on to Guangzhou. In each of the cities of Guangzhou, Shanghai and Beijing ring roads have been constructed. In some cases, three rings encircle the cities. Similar programs are being developed throughout the urban area of China. Many of these projects are joint ventures with U.S. or European companies and part of the plan to complete 30,000 kilometers of toll road throughout the country.

Illustration 5: A Typical Rural Segment of Newly Opened Highway

The United States Transportation Plan

What is our plan to compete with these two trading blocks that will allow the U.S. to compete? What revenue stream will be used to design and construct the necessary transportation capacity? What are the U.S. plans for establishing regional rail passenger service or other mass transit systems? Is there a plan for transportation that stimulates the economy and provides the necessary funding to do so? Do these plans establish a connection between use and cost that will balance revenue generation with demand in a system of economic decision making?

Absent plans for transportation that include funding and pricing, eighty seven per cent of the value of all freight moved in the United States is moved on the highway and the automobile continues to reign supreme. We are seeing a reduced percentage of the total passenger trips being taken on transit and these trends appear to be continuing. The lack of pricing is causing an imbalance in demand and could be leading to significant negative consequences.

In the interim, we are preoccupied with the allocation of existing revenues. Constituencies of various interests are attempting to influence lawmakers to allocate a greater proportion of funding to programs or geographic areas. States that contribute more of the federal gasoline tax than they receive are consistently lobbying for more of the taxes collected in their states to be returned to their states. Those states that receive more than they contribute, attempt to maintain the status quo. Proponents of rail and bus transit modes lobby for more of the available revenue to be allocated those programs. Highway advocates lobby to maintain funding for highway maintenance and construction programs and the preservation of the trust fund. While these maneuvers continue, other stakeholders pursue earmarks "off the top" before allocation. Congressmen who possess seniority and sit on key transportation committees try to provide for their constituents by bringing home federal dollars for projects identified as high priority by their local officials and metropolitan planning organizations. In a Congress designed for a balance of power based on population (House of Representatives) and status as a state (Senate), it is difficult to pass a funding package at all.

Tradition also plays a role in the allocation of funds for highways. The system of collecting and allocating gas tax has been a part of funding transportation since 1916. It is difficult to alter such systems of practice, bureaucracy and political power. While sweeping changes may seem appropriate and even necessary, it is unlikely with so much tradition and procedure. Modifications and incremental change are most likely if implemented through systems of government rather than through economic means. Those involved in bureaucracy and the politically powerful would certainly oppose changes that reduce their ability to influence and control.

While it is perhaps wise to transition transportation funding processes, incremental changes aid those wishing to maintain the status quo. Momentum for change seems unjustified from a parochial perspective especially if the cycle of allocations is due to bless your state or interest group.

Some have advocated a complete change in the methods of funding transportation that include elimination of the gasoline tax and implementing a system that will charge for each mile traveled. While probably technically possible, from a political viewpoint it is unlikely and perhaps unwise. Such wholesale change might reap enormous unintended consequences. Transportation funding influences the economic, political and social fabric of a nation and at the least, a federal policy framework for transportation will be difficult if not impossible to maintain. It certainly seems logical to charge for the exact use of the surface transportation system but the complete repeal of gasoline tax will require a new bureaucracy of collection and a renewed and perhaps fierce debate over how money collected, by which level of government, how funds will be returned to the states and localities and reverberating government program impacts are likely.

Complementary systems of transportation funding and operation seem most reasonable, least disruptive and most probable to succeed in altering the policy focus to transportation needs rather than the allocation of existing funds. Careful planning for a transition to new methods of collection and distribution will minimize disruptions to the transportation system and unintended economic impacts.

The effects of a complete change in transportation funding methods should be considered within the policy framework of transportation. Of course, a surface transportation system has economic ramifications and purpose but there are social implications as well. Transportation is at once a public good and, in some regards, a private one. Portions of the surface transportation system are funded through property taxes and other general purpose taxes and serve a general public access purpose. The local surface transportation system serves various trip purposes such as school, medical, recreational etc. The arterial system however, is funded through gasoline taxes and serves a predominant economic purpose. What taxation or pricing scheme is appropriate for all of the surface transportation system? Does a per mile charge for the local trip serve the same policy purpose as the long haul freight trip? Perhaps no system of charging is appropriate for all the transportation system.

Imagine a system in which concessionaires construct major interstate and arterial highways, as is the case in Europe. The process of awarding concessions serves to complement existing fund allocation processes for public projects. These concessions are designed to economically support themselves from project revenue and are operated by the private sector. Lower volume projects that serve the purpose of access to transportation or projects that are too costly to support strictly from the revenue stream are either supplemented with public funds or built exclusively with public funds.

If such a system were used on all arterial projects in the U.S., methods of selecting construction firms might change and perhaps, the form contractual arrangements would alter. No longer would construction be awarded on the basis of a public procurement or a low bid method. The concessionaire would select the construction company or may, in fact, have their own construction company. While this process may be sufficient it is nevertheless significantly different from current procedure and accepted practice.

Such change would likely be resisted and huge modifications in process would be required. Bureaucracies that currently control the fund allocation and administration process would lose a great deal of control and the federal gasoline tax that is currently sent to Washington for redistribution would cease and the ability to set nationwide transportation policy would be hampered.

The next two chapters will begin to unravel these quandaries and offer some possibilities for all to participate in reinventing transportation in the United States.

4

We are continually faced with a series of great opportunities brilliantly disguised as insoluble problems.

—*John W. Gardner*

DISSECTING THE CHALLENGES OF TRANSPORTATION

How often have we instituted solutions to modern day issues, only to determine during implementation that we are solving the wrong problem? This is particularly true when attempting to resolve the challenges of transportation. Transportation is not an amorphous, conglomerate concept but is composed of many facets. Good intentions and an inclusive approach have precipitated a view of transportation as a single issue. We tend to discuss transportation as inclusive of all modes and circumstances. However, it is not useful to analyze transportation challenges as a total system, multi-modal, intermodal, concept it must be analyzed in components. Dividing the issue of transportation into its component parts makes the questions more discrete and understandable, and avoids the confusion introduced by broad statements.

For example, transportation conclusions reached in sparsely populated rural areas of the United States may not be assumed to be applicable in Manhattan. Conclusions about passenger travel may not be applicable to freight. It is reasonable to debate the analysis approach and what components of transportation should be isolated for analysis but attempting to analyze transportation as an single policy question has limited practical value.

Sometimes transportation policy analysis is performed in such a way that preference and bias is introduced. On occasion analysts, lobbyists, politicians and the public will incorporate solutions into the definition of the question. Our preferences for modal choice or our desire to meet business objectives may affect the way in which we choose analyze data or segment the issue. For example, a policy preference for moving freight by rail might result in an analysis of freight movement being expressed in tons or ton-miles; if the preference is for air freight, question may be analyzed in terms of the value of freight moved or the travel time. Question definition should more properly be based upon the public purpose of the transportation activity rather than the transportation solution or mode of transportation employed.

What are the components of transportation that should be considered in devising surface transportation policy? Transportation provides the public purpose of access but also serves the private purpose of economic commerce. Just as urban and rural transportation environments differ, freight transportation and passenger movement are uniquely different. Passenger service is commonly accomplished by private automobile and freight movement through a business enterprise and the manner in which transportation decisions are made varies for the two sectors. Rights and privacy considerations weigh heavily for the individual, while freight companies are more concerned with profitability and time sensitive deliveries.

There are, of course, modal choices within each of these sectors. That is, passenger travel may be accomplished using the automobile, bus, rail, water or air. Similar modal choices are available to the freight sector. However, modal choice will likely be made on quite different criteria for the two sectors. To provide some segmentation of the transportation policy question, it seems appropriate to identify freight and passenger as separate components of the larger transportation issue. Just as freight and passenger service are unique components of the transportation question, the purpose and need for transportation is unique between urban and rural environments.

Urbanization of the United States has created new challenges for transportation planning. Urban concentrations of residences, business centers, and shopping areas have occurred in such a way as to expand cities into large metro areas. While residences are concentrated, they are not in close proximity to business centers and this has contributed to the generation of large numbers of trips in urban areas. In addition, the purpose of urban trips has become more shopping, recreational and non commute in nature. However, growth has continued to be patterned on economics and the expansion of urban areas into ever larger suburban, metropolitan regions has led to peak demands for transportation services and hence tremendous challenges. The urban metropolitan areas contrast with the needs for transportation in the rural areas where the primary issue is access. Access to schools, shopping, church, medical care, and jobs is an increasing need in rural America, especially as urbanization continues and the median age of the population increases.

Freight and passenger travel in the urban and rural environments provide a reasonable matrix for analyzing transportation policy. The areas of inquiry chosen for analysis are therefore urban-freight, urban-passenger, rural-freight and rural-passenger. The definition of an urban area should be accepted as defined in federal legislation, a contiguous metropolitan area with a population greater than 50,000.

Many factors affect transportation decision making across the four chosen sectors of transportation. Some of these are organization, finance, and political tradition. Finance will however drive many of the aspects of transportation policy and decision making. Each of the transportation segments identified has evolved predominantly in the last century as the transportation infrastructure was built in support of urbanization and growing economic activity. The century began with building roads to support mobility via the new automobile and ended with the completion of the interstate system. The financial aspects of transportation were driven by the primary funding mechanism, the gasoline tax. In the last five to ten years questions have arisen as to its adequacy and relevance.

Inherent in the issue of funding transportation is the question of who pays and who benefits. Is transportation predominantly a public service/good that all in society should benefit from equally or is transportation a private good that should be paid for based on direct use? Is the solution to price all who use transportation for the use? Will the pricing schemes be adequate to generate sufficient revenue for transportation? If pricing is introduced will it modify consumptive behavior? These questions and the appropriate conclusions range across the four analysis sectors chosen and must be considered separately.

Pricing Transportation and the Gasoline Tax

If we consider transportation as a public good or commodity, how do we and how should we set a price for transportation that assures equitable access and adequate supply? Consider the approach in the United States. First, the cost to use transportation, at least in the case of roadways, is perceived to be zero. What is the cost to use the roadway annually, daily, per trip or on any other measure? Few users of the transportation system could answer such questions, and are unaware of the intricacies involved in financing public roadways. Though the gasoline tax has been the primary funding mechanism for transportation, few of the general population and even the transportation professions, are aware of the rate at which gasoline is taxed. The conscious connection between use and cost in personal transportation decision making has been lost. There exists no metering of demand based on cost as there is with electricity, water or other public utilities.

The federal gasoline tax rate in the United States is 18.4 cents per gallon. Added to the federal gasoline tax is the state gasoline tax with rates that range from 7.5 cents/gallon to 31.3 cents/gallon. The average state gasoline tax rate is 21.6 cents/gallon. The table below presents gasoline tax rates by state.[70]

Table 17: Motor Fuel Tax Rates by State

State	Cents/gal.	State	Cents/gal.
Alabama	18	Montana	27.75
Alaska	8	Nebraska	24.6
Arizona	18	Nevada	23
Arkansas	21.5	New Hampshire	18
California	18	New Jersey	14.5
Colorado	22	New Mexico	17
Connecticut	25	New York	29.65
Delaware	23	North Carolina	23.4
D.C.	20	North Dakota	21
Florida	14.1	Ohio	22
Georgia	7.5	Oklahoma	17
Hawaii	16	Oregon	24
Idaho	25	Pennsylvania	25.9
Illinois	19	Rhode Island	30
Indiana	18	South Carolina	16
Iowa	20.1	South Dakota	22
Kansas	23	Tennessee	20
Kentucky	15	Texas	20
Louisiana	20	Utah	24.5
Maine	22	Vermont	20
Maryland	23.5	Virginia	17.5

Table 17: Motor Fuel Tax Rates by State (Continued)

State	Cents/gal.	State	Cents/gal.
Massachusetts	21.5	Washington	23
Michigan	19	West Virginia	20.5
Minnesota	20	Wisconsin	31.1
Mississippi	18	Wyoming	14
Missouri	17	Federal Tax	18.4

In comparison to some other developed countries, the tax rates of the United States are an order of magnitude lower. The table below shows gasoline tax rates and diesel fuel tax rates converted to equivalent cents/gallon in September 2001[71].

Table 18: Motor Fuel Tax Rates for Select Countries

COUNTRY	GASOLINE	DIESEL
Belgium	226	145
France	249	171
Germany	247	176
Italy	241	185
Netherlands	265	160
United Kingdom	309	313
Japan	175	110
United States	38	44

It is immediately evident that other countries of the world have been pricing the use of automobiles at a much higher level. Many of these countries have also chosen not to dedicate gasoline tax to transportation but place proceeds in the general fund. Consequently, transportation initiatives must compete with other general fund initiatives during annual appropriations cycles. Whether the purpose of this taxation level is revenue generation or pricing of a public good to affect public demand, some behavioral aspects are evident.

A casual observation of vehicles in the United States versus these of other developed countries would suggest there has been some economic effect on vehicle choice. Vehicle choice in the United States seems to bear no relationship to economics. In fact, the entire growth in personal vehicles over the last decade in the United States has been in light-duty trucks (i.e., vans and SUVs). At the very least fuel tax rates would seem to have an impact on vehicle choice.

Fuel tax rates might have a cause and effect relationship to development densities. There are historical, cultural and other reasons that more dense urban development patterns exist in Europe. However, higher costs for travel by automobile might affect the economic decisions that result in suburbanization. An argument could also be made that higher gasoline tax rates affect modal choice. Whatever the policy implications, it remains clear that the United States lags all developed countries in gasoline tax rates and therefore in its ability to influence the demand for transportation.

In those countries where gasoline tax proceeds are used for other than transportation, gasoline taxes are viewed more as a general tax than a user fee. In addition to gasoline tax, many European countries levy taxes on the purchase price of a vehicle that exceed the price of the vehicle by a factor of two. Further, the European arterial highway systems are funded from tolls levied by concessionaires. Governments grant these concessions, typically, for a period of thirty years. These arterial highway are similar to the interstate system in the U.S. which was funded through gasoline tax. The contrast between Europe and U.S. transportation funding methods provides a back drop for the greatly differing economic choices made by users of transportation.

Canada has a tax rate schedule similar to the United States. It has the next lowest gasoline tax to the United States. Japan also has a lower gasoline tax rate but it is still nearly four times that of the United States. Canada has provincial tax rates that vary from 34 cents Canadian per U.S. gallon in Alberta to 70 cents Canadian per gallon in Newfoundland.[72] This is in addition to a Canadian federal gasoline tax rate of ten cents per liter or about 38 cents Canadian per gallon. After converting for exchange rate, the total Canadian tax is about $.55 per gallon.

While gasoline tax is stated to be a user fee, in most developed countries of the world it more resembles a general tax. In the United States it is at least a surrogate of a direct user fee and probably the best substitute available at the time. The term "user fee" implies a relationship between the production of surface transportation supply and demand. However, even though the U.S. gasoline tax is dedicated in trust funds, it represents only a small portion of the real cost incurred for transportation. A complete cost analysis should, of course, include the cost of providing the roadways but they should also include the environmental costs that result from the predominance of the automobile as a modal choice. Data would suggest however that taxation rates are insufficient to even cover the costs of providing highway infrastructure.

Assuming a fleet fuel efficiency of 20 miles per gallon, which is near the corporate average fuel economy (CAFÉ) standards for the United States, and a tax rate of 38 cents per gallon; the cost per mile is 38/20, or about 1.9 cents per mile for gasoline tax. This represents essentially the price charged for construction, maintenance and operation of the highway system. This calculation for an average European tax rate of $2.50 per gallon would be 12.5 cents per mile. Further, if travel takes place on an arterial highway in Europe, there are tolls to be paid and these would average a similar amount or a total of 25 cents per mile. One thousand miles per month would $19.00 per month in the United States and $125.00 per month in Europe. If this travel occurs on the arterial system of Europe, the monthly amount would be $250.00.

The highway cost incurred by a driver in the U.S. are small in comparison to other costs they incur. The full operating costs incurred by the individual are much higher than those imposed by the fuel tax. The largest component of that cost is depreciation. The full cost of operating an automobile is evident in car rental rates. The rates must be sufficient to recover the full cost plus profit. Consider a new SUV at a price of $35,000 and an average of 15,000 miles per year for three years. Assuming depreciation over three years of $17,500 or half of the vehicles value, the depreciation rate of such a vehicle on a per mile basis would be 39 cents per mile. This is considerably greater than the 1.9 cents per mile of fuel tax. Including other costs, such as maintenance, insurance, etc., full-cost rental rates would be approximately 50 cents. As a nation we are therefore willing to pay 25 times more per mile for the vehicle in the United States than for the roadway upon which we ride.

Matching Transportation Funding and Needs

In the United States the supply or capacity of transportation is restricted to what can be built with the revenue available. Remember that the public perception is that the price is zero. Clearly, a commodity that has a perceived price of zero has unlimited demand in the marketplace and yet we are surprised that we can not build sufficient capacity to satisfy the growth in use. Our transportation pricing policies lead us to this result. Truly, we can not build our way out of the congestion that we are experiencing unless we can build an unlimited capacity or perhaps modify transportation pricing to meter demand.

How is the proper level of supply determined to meet demand? We currently do so by allocating funds available and calculating the unsatisfied need for additional transportation. This approach is inadequate on its face. We also allocate funds, however, based upon agendas other than documented need. For example, federal funds are still allocated on the basis of rural postal service routes as well as a host of factors, including roadway mileage, land area and population, all of which are surrogates of the need for additional transportation capacity.

Fund allocation has also become a method to ensure compliance with various policies. Withholding of funds was threatened for many years unless motorcycle helmet laws were enacted and enforced at the state level. The same was true for the 55 speed limit, drunk driving and others. While the benefit to the public of these requirements may have been positive, they are nevertheless unrelated to need for transportation funding.

Funds at all levels of government are also allocated to encourage various modes of transportation. Currently 2.86 cents of the 18.4 cent federal gasoline tax is devoted to mass transit, approximately 15.5 per cent. In many states, similar allocation levels have been established for state-funded transportation expenditures. Some states might require significantly more than 15.5 per cent for mass transit; states that are sparsely populated would have less mass transit needs. The issue in question is not whether one transportation mode offers more efficiency than another, but that funds are distributed based on predetermined percentages that may or may not be sufficient to satisfy the need for transportation facilities, either for transit or highways.

In addition to allocating transportation funding for various policy agendas, funds are also appropriated at the federal and state levels for specific projects. Politicians use this as a way to bypass allocation processes and ensure that their chosen projects are funded. Such approaches may provide funding to the highest priority projects, however the criteria of selection are not focused on need but rather their worth as political bargaining chips.

If unfunded transportation projects exist, how can they be identified and how should they be prioritized? Professionals in the transportation field identify transportation needs on the basis of sufficiency, capacity and safety. Capacity is based upon the design capacity of the thoroughfare minus current traffic volumes. Safety is measured by analyzing a myriad of accident statistics centered on fatalities, injuries and property damage. While capacity and, to a lesser extent, safety criteria are straightforward, sufficiency is unique to transportation. It is basically an assessment of the overall adequacy of the roadway or bridge to handle demand. In effect it is a measure of the roadway's adequacy based upon accepted standards for design. These three criteria are the foundation for determining needs and involve numerical calculations based on accident statistics, projections of traffic growth and highway design. A cost-benefit calculation is the final priority-setting calculation.

The process becomes enormously more difficult when prioritizing projects across jurisdictional boundaries or facility types. Of the substantial transportation needs that exist, which ones should get the funding first? When we add jurisdictional wishes into the decision-making process, it is apparent how difficult is the task. Each jurisdiction wants the funding of its projects first. This is true at the state level, within the states at the metropolitan level and within the metropolitan regions between competing cities and counties. This process has been further complicated by the well intentioned desire to encourage more local input.

An organization that has had a significant impact on the fund allocation and prioritization process is the Metropolitan Planning Organization, MPO. The federal Intermodal Surface Transportation Efficiency Act (ISTEA) passed in 1991, assumed that by creating metropolitan planning agencies local officials would have greater input into prioritizing projects and that transportation would be better coordinated with land use at the local level. The legislation required that an MPO be designated for urban areas with more than 50,000 population and further that the governor of each state agree with the member designation. Guidelines required that the "units of general purpose local government, which together represent 75 percent of the affected population."[73] The net effect has been that state transportation agencies that were previously responsible for setting priorities based upon the criteria of capacity, safety and sufficiency are now required to accept input of local metropolitan planning agencies. Certainly state agencies considered political input previously but with the greater involvement of MPOs in the prioritization process, state agency influence has decreased. In some cases, the result appears to be a near abdication of responsibility by the state DOTs in favor of a local politically charged process.

Insufficient funds, large numbers of categories of funding that limit which projects can receive federal funding and other factors could result in projects being delayed. As this occurred, local officials became very dissatisfied if money was not programmed to their favorite project and consequently state DOTs have been more than willing to pass some of the responsibility on to the MPO. In effect, this has given state transportation agencies the option to abdicate prioritization responsibility and share the discontent with those same local officials. While the majority of state statutes have preserved the state DOT's authority to program funds to projects, the priorities are set by the local MPOs. In summary, the increased role of the MPOs outlined in ISTEA in 1991 has allowed a further devolution of the allocation process that has become even more political. The result is a tendency away from data analysis representing the needs for projects to political prioritization based upon public surveys of desire or other local agendas. Though technical committees of transportation professionals are assigned the task of providing for capacity, safety and sufficiency factors, the deliberations are similar to the political discussions of the full MPO. Cities and counties are avid advocates for their projects and that advocacy is apparent in the technical committee meetings. The work by MPO technical committees, required by legislation is therefore commonly usurped by the local political process.

A Theoretical Framework for Transportation

A theoretical framework for this decision-making quandary is the seminal work of James Buchanan in his book Public Economics.[74] The essence of the concept of public economics applied to transportation would imply that transportation demand should be expressed as a preference curve that the citizenry has for public goods. It is the price they are willing to pay to share in a public good.

An example of a "pure" public good might be national defense. It is something that each of us can share without detracting from the next citizen's ability to be defended. Most public goods, however, are not "pure." Generically we think of public goods as those that are best provided by government for the benefit of all the citizenry. Unlike defense, the use of a public good such as transportation detracts from the next citizen's ability to use the same transportation facility. This is particularly true for transportation during peak hours when we all want to use the roadway at the same time. Public economic theory would predict that we each have different preferences for public goods and that some are more willing or able to pay for those goods. The use of gasoline tax as the primary transportation funding mechanism makes the price of transportation the same for all of us regardless of when we use the transportation facility. Gasoline taxes offer no method for us to register our preference for transportation. A direct user fee system would offer that opportunity.

The concept of public and private goods can be clarified by considering the hypothetical example of a swimming pool. The public attributes of the swimming pool are directly related to the pricing for use and the size or supply of the good. Assume that the swimming pool is located in an exclusive country club. The initiation fee for the country club membership is $50,000 plus a minimum of $200 per month must be spent at the club for entertainment. A membership permits unlimited use of the swimming pool for a family and a maximum of two guests at a time. Such a swimming pool would undoubtedly have the traits of a private good. There would be no issues with the size of the pool and therefore the supply of the good. After a time, the city decides to buy the country club and make the facilities more accessible to the public. There initiation fee is eliminated and there is no requirement for minimum entertainment expenses, but there is a fee of $10 per person for each time the pool is used. While the pool is more accessible to the general public, it could still be viewed as demonstrating many of the traits of a private good. The pool has not reached its capacity but there are many more people using the pool. Upon further deliberations of the city fathers, it is determined that the fee for use of the pool should be eliminated. Now the pool is used to its maximum capacity and, on warm days, the pool is forced to close because it is over capacity. The pool now demonstrates the attributes of a public good in all but one aspect, capacity is not sufficient for all citizens to enjoy the pool.

This example illustrates how the attributes of a particular good can change based upon access and pricing. The same swimming pool changed from an exclusively private good to a public good. There is, however, the necessity to price the product at a level sufficient to balance supply and demand and to generate sufficient revenue to increase capacity.

This theoretical framework of public choice is coming into practice in the transportation field in the form of high occupant toll roads, variable pricing, congestion pricing, demand pricing and other price-for-use concepts. These techniques give the user the option of receiving higher levels of service for increased cost and the ability to register their preferences with the payment of the higher toll.

Urban Passenger Travel

Urban passenger travel is usually what we think of when debating the questions of transportation. Peak-hour traffic congestion during the home-to-work trip is well understood by citizens who experience the event on a daily basis. Traffic congestion is so severe in many urban areas, that the trip to work has become a time to apply cosmetics, eat meals or even read the newspaper. The National Highway and Traffic Safety Administration estimates that 25 per cent of police-reported crashes involve some form of driver inattention. What has led us to this condition?

After World War II several events conspired to create the urban passenger travel dilemma. With military men returning home, marriages skyrocketed and a boom in home purchases occurred. This was amplified by low-interest loans and low down payments made possible by several government programs for veterans. Many dreamed of a yard with a picket fence, a pleasant peaceful environment away from the noise and troubles of the city and the result was aggressive suburbanization. From 1940 to 1990 the number of housing units increased from 37 million to 102 million, a 173 per cent increase. At the same time the percentage of houses located in the suburb rose from 19 per cent of total housing to 44 per cent, housing in central cities reduced from 34 per cent to 32 per cent and outside metro areas declined from 46 per cent to 24 per cent.[75] Growth occurred around the cities where the jobs were and peak-hour travel increased. Over time community services developed in the suburbs, and groceries, gardening supplies, home improvement, other businesses began to find a market in the suburbs. Today, urban passenger travel is very different. The primary trip purpose has expanded from home-to-work to include shopping, recreation, education, etc. Most suburban trips in major metropolitan areas now start and end in the suburb. The frequency of the typical trip has also increased. Today, planners estimate trip generation using the standard of ten trips per household per day.

The automobile is the principal vehicle of choice in the urban areas of the United States, but the last ten years have seen large changes in the types of vehicles. As presented earlier, the number of automobiles in the United States in 1990 was nearly equivalent to the number in 2000,[76] approximately 133 million. Other two-axle four-tire vehicles increased in the same period, however, from 48 million to 79 million. The urban vehicle of choice has become a low-mileage, more polluting, heavier vehicle in the form of vans and sport utility vehicles (SUVs).

The home-to-work trip length has also increased in the United States as the expansion of metropolitan areas has continued. The farther out that the metropolitan traveler must go to find affordable homes and a suburban life style, the longer the daily commute. From 1983 to 2001 the average trip length in urban areas has increased from 8.5 miles to 12.4 and for trips not in the urban area the commute length has increased from 8.6 to 22.6[77]

This growth in trip length has changed how urban roadways are used. The interstate system was designed and built for national defense purposes, but also to connect the major urban centers of the United States. The system was literally for "interstate travel." As the system was substantially completing, the suburbanization of America was occurring. Many more of the trips on the interstate system were becoming urban commuting trips and then suburb-to-suburb trips. The use of the interstate highway in urban areas changed from interstate in purpose to urban/suburban/regional in nature. Some would argue that the presence of interstate highways in urban areas, particularly beltways, further intensified suburbanization.

Though the interstate highway system was built with 90 per cent federal and 10 per cent state funds, in the urban area it became a system of urban arterials; the major urban thoroughfares of the United States. Is it any wonder that Congressman and Senators wanted to add beltways around large cities in their respective congressional districts? As interstate highway passenger traffic increased and truck freight traffic increased, beltways were built to keep interstate travel away from city centers. But, they also served to create broader sub-urbanization and longer commute trips. The beltways that were added to the interstate definition before 1973 increased urban high-volume capacity. Because of Congressional action to limit the addition of mileage to the interstate system definition additions to the interstate system ceased and some urban areas funded expressways through tolling. As interstate capacity continued to be built over the last thirty years, further suburbanization, commercial development, and longer trip lengths was the result. Additionally, passenger cars intermingled with growing truck freight traffic and the cycle of congestion continued.

Urban Freight Movement

Three primary factors affect the amount of freight traffic in an urban area: presence of population, industry and intermodal facilities. Obviously the presence of population creates the need for goods movement. Even though 80 per cent of the United States Gross Domestic Product (GDP) is generated through the provision of services, urban areas still need food, clothing, other consumables and durable goods such as cars, home appliances and furniture. Construction materials and equipment and many other products that make up the basics of economic life must be transported in the urban area.

The presence of industry, whether manufacturing, assembly, energy or other industry; amplifies the freight trips expected in an urban area. Each of these industries is a large generator and/or attractor of urban freight trips. This concentration of urban freight traffic added to the growth in automobile traffic merely serves to heighten congestion. Local industrial freight trips add to freight trips that are passing through the urban area to another destination on the interstate.

The third factor affecting the volume of urban freight trips is the presence of a major intermodal facility. Most of the larger cities of America were originally located based upon geographical features that made transportation possible; usually a river, bay, lake or other physical feature. Occasionally, these geographical features were also demarcations of international borders. These ports served as intermodal freight centers in moving goods regionally, nationally and internationally.

Other, less evident intermodal centers resulted from the dependence upon the highway or rail for freight movement in the United States rather than from a geographical feature. Kansas City, Cheyenne, Denver and other major urban areas grew from the establishment of rail heads for moving freight between the eastern and western halves of the United States during the rail era of the nineteenth century.

In more recent times, major intermodal facilities have developed as major land ports. These are geographically convenient locations, near interstate highways, where loads can be combined or separated for distribution to a regional area. They are not so different from seaports or major rail heads where loads are assembled for sea or rail transport. These land ports are typified by large warehousing operations.

As demonstrated earlier, the cost-per-mile efficiency of the truck is not the chief reason for choosing to transport by truck. Many other modes offer better raw efficiency, but a truck's flexibility avoids unnecessary loading and unloading and, therefore, keeps total transit time to a minimum. Additionally, the truck is much better suited to the urban environment as a freight delivery system. For rail freight delivery to be effective, switching facilities, loading equipment and rail spurs are required. Such facilities take up large tracts of land and cannot be cost effectively located near the final destination, usually an urban destination.

As described earlier, growth in truck freight movement has been dramatically affected by the deregulation of trucking in the United States and by the North American Free Trade Agreement. These two events and the greater flexibility exhibited by trucks, have combined to make truck freight movement dominant. This is particularly evident in the urban area. Over the last twenty years, many urban rail spurs have been abandoned and many of these abandoned tracks have been converted to other purposes including bicycle trails under "rails to trails" programs set out in federal ISTEA legislation. This program allows federal transportation funds to be used for converting abandoned rail lines to bicycle and pedestrian trails.

In the nineteenth century, transportation was predominantly provided by the railroads and towns grew up around the stops, some of which became the cities of today. It was extremely practical to have rails running through the middle of the town when rail was the predominant mode of surface transportation. With the exception of major industries with long-established rail access, the delivery of freight by rail is not competitive in today's just-in-time business environment but the rail lines remain and create traffic delay at intersections with roadways.

Most rail lines are privately owned and operated and cities have begun to realize that freight lines in urban areas can introduce inefficiency to the entire transportation system because of the many railroad crossings. The Alameda Corridor project in the Los Angeles area was constructed to remove 200 railroad grade crossings in the Los Angeles area and is estimated to save 15,000 hours of vehicle delay per day. The project consolidated three rail lines into one high capacity rail line and eliminates all at-grade railroad crossings in the corridor.[78] The project connects the major seaports of Los Angeles and Long Beach to a freight intermodal transfer center. Approximately one quarter of all products arriving in the United States moves through these two ports.[79] Through innovative financing using federal loan guarantees, a proposal was devised for a grade-separated rail line reconstruction that runs twenty miles through an urban area to a rail head, intermodal staging facility. From the intermodal staging area, outside the urban core, freight is transported by rail or trucks to its final destination.

Other cities have considered the relocation of rail freight lines from the city center to outlying suburban areas. Others have considered using existing rail lines for light rail or commuter rail passenger service. Because the freight lines are privately owned, there is no sound economic reason to expend funds to move the urban lines. In fact, some industries located in urban areas would be forced to relocate themselves if rail lines ceased to operate.

Air freight has become a growing component in urban freight movement and has stimulated ground traffic in and around major airports. Freight moved by air is primarily long-distance, high-value, low volume and low weight. The cut flower, mail delivery and small parcel delivery industries have seen large growth. Because of this airports are becoming intermodal freight centers surrounded by large warehousing operations for local and regional distribution. Air freight is not likely to compete with surface transportation for major portions of the freight market but the presence of the growing air freight market in urban areas stimulates many ground trips in a concentrated area as freight is unloaded, perhaps repackaged, and reloaded for ultimate distribution. The Bureau of Transportation Statistics reports that airports accounted for only 3 per cent of the value of freight in 1997 and .2 per cent of the ton-miles of freight. This sector of freight movement will also be stimulated by the retail activity taking place on the Internet.

Rural Passenger Transportation

Passenger travel in the rural areas of the United States has shown some signs of congestion, in particular on major interstate routes, but rural passenger transportation in the United States is predominantly an issue of access, especially for elderly populations. Access to medical care, emergency services, food and other life sustaining necessities are major concerns for many in rural areas. These trips tend to be short, except in the expansive, sparsely populated western states, and play a relatively minor economic role. Longer rural passenger trips are those of most interest from an economic perspective and essentially represent connections between metropolitan areas.

Historically, interurban trips were accommodated by the rail system. With the advent of the automobile and later the airline, rail has declined to a miniscule percentage of the rural passenger trips once handled by rail. With the construction of the interstate highway system the automobile, and to a lesser extent, the bus, provided most of the intercity mobility. While there have been attempts to maintain long-distance rail passenger service through the establishment and continued funding of Amtrak, it is a service that must compete with the speed of air travel and the convenience of the automobile. Airline travel has captured the majority of the travel market more than 500 miles in length and the automobile have captured the shorter distances leaving little market for rail except in very densely populated corridors.

Automobile travel in the last half of the twentieth century went from 587 billion vehicle miles traveled in 1960 to 1.659 trillion in 2002 and was concurrent with the growth of domestic commercial air travel.[80] With the terrible events of 9/11/2001, air passenger travel reduced but has essentially returned to previous levels. The balance between air travel and the automobile however does seem to have been altered somewhat. In 2001 business air travel expenditures were 16.5 per cent less than in 2000.[81]

Security requirements for passengers and baggage have been the lasting impact of 9/11 and have altered the time savings and convenience of air travel. The trip distance at which air travel becomes more efficient and convenient has lengthened. The choice between air and automobile travel is quite different for business than for pleasure but the choice between the automobile and air travel has altered somewhat resulting in more rural passenger trips on the highway. A trip of 300 miles by automobile begins to be a better choice with the time required to go through the security screening. It is also more convenient and flexible to travel by automobile in terms of scheduling the time of travel. Whatever the distance, the time efficiency of air travel has been slightly altered in favor of the automobile.

Rural Freight

As previously established, rail is not a competitive transportation mode except for heavy bulk, low-value freight. The lightest and most valuable freight is transported by air where the average value of freight is $38 per lb.[82] Those commodities that lie between are typically transported by truck. An increasingly limiting factor in long-distance truck freight has become congestion. The vast majority of this intercity truck freight movement takes place on the interstate highway system and other major arterial highways. Some sections of rural interstate highways have become increasingly congested, and this suggests the potential for safety issues as well as economic concerns.

However, congestion in the urban areas of the United States has become a major impediment to long-distance truck freight movement. Many interstate routes pass through the heart of major cities and the capacity available for intercity freight movement is being consumed by local urban travel. As the hours of peak travel congestion expand, there is less probability that an intercity freight hauler will be able to pass through the city without delay. The original purpose of the routes was for long-distance intercity travel, but they have become urban arterials serving predominantly urban trips. Although beltways have been constructed around many metropolitan areas, suburbanization has begun to congest as well. Navigating through urban areas has become a limiting factor in long distance freight movement by truck.

It would seem that with the increasing impact of urban congestion on intercity freight movement, that rail would become a more attractive alternative. While it might be fuel efficient to encourage long-distance freight movement on the rail systems of the United States, it is likely that the truck will continue to dominate because of the need to disassemble and assemble trains at various points along the trip. Projections of rural freight traffic made by the Federal Highway Administration, Motor Carrier Division indicate that by 2020 35 per cent of the rural interstate highways will have 10,000 or more tractor-trailer vehicles per day and 65 percent of the urban interstate highways will exceed that number.[83] The following maps of the United States present the truck volumes on the nation's highways in 1998 and for 2020. The thin lines are 5,000 per day, thicker lines are 5,000 to 10,000 per day and the thickest lines represent over 10,000 per day. Clearly, the increase is significant.

Ten thousand tractor trailer trucks per day will have an enormous impact on the congestion patterns of urban areas. These vehicles accelerate and brake at very different rates from those of the typical automobile. In stop and go traffic the larger number of heavy vehicles will respond much more slowly and congestion will increase safety concerns.

Illustration 6: Truck Volumes 1998

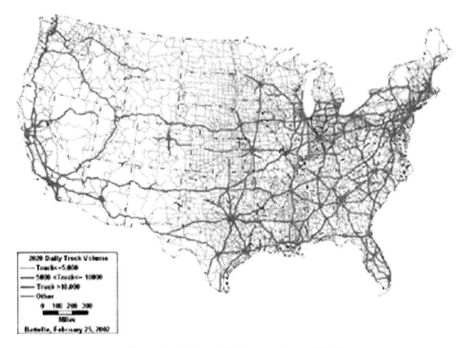

Illustration 7: Truck Volumes Projected 2020

Secure Freight Movement and Transportation Efficiency

The awful events of 9/11 heightened the concern for security in the U.S. and much has been accomplished to apply various technologies to freight clearance. Whether moving freight through international ports, across international borders or through a city, freight security has become a significant issue. Though much has been done with regard to passenger security, freight security represents a major potential vulnerability to homeland security. The enormous and growing volume of freight moving across the vastness of America or arriving at international boundaries or seaports is growing concern. The economic impact of security in air passenger transportation has been considerable and a similar result could occur in the area of freight security.

Security in freight movement involves three components, identification of the freight being moved, the vehicle, and the operator and all must be tracked with certainty to maintain a secure motor freight operation. While many freight security issues exist, the application of Global Positioning Satellite (GPS) technology to transportation offers an overall framework for tracking location. When applications are developed to integrate information about the vehicle, operator and cargo to GPS freight security will become less of a security concern. However, freight entering the country is a concern that should receive immediate attention.

A potential threat to American security is at seaports. While it is unrealistic to inspect all cargo imported to the United States, much can be accomplished with today's technology to improve security and simultaneously improve the efficiency of cargo movement. It has long been recognized by the transportation industry that the efficiency of intermodal centers can significantly affect the overall efficiency of the transportation system. Also, these centers are coincident with freight security activity. Freight transfer operations can be the bottlenecks that restrict an otherwise fast moving transportation system and security procedures could hamper that efficiency. With the passage of the intermodal surface transportation efficiency act (ISTEA) in 1991, intermodalism has been center stage in the transportation policy of the United States. With the technology developed in the tolling and ITS markets, the opportunity exists that would allow the accomplishment of these two seemingly conflicting goals.

Advanced technology exists throughout the transportation industry that could be applied to the freight transfer and security dilemma. Electronic toll collection has revolutionized the toll industry and similar RFID technology has begun to be widely used in pallet tracking. These technologies offer an extraordinary foundation for building freight security systems. Entire cargoes and pallets of freight can be tracked and the location recorded by various RFID readers along the route and particularly through the transfer location. Technology companies have even developed readers that are embedded in belts which are worn by the individuals handling freight pallets. This process allows segments of cargo that are assembled into trailer loads to be tracked throughout the transfer and hauling process.

Other technologies exist to scan cargoes with ion scanners and X-rays and thereby determine the presence of explosives or check bills of lading against X-ray profiles. Vehicle operators can be tracked with infrared technology and identification systems and such systems are plentiful and widely accepted. Vehicles can be profiled with laser technology identifying various vehicle types and loads entering and exiting the ports and license plate recognition technology can identify and record vehicle registration. The integration of these technologies would automate the identification of the cargo, the vehicle and the individual operator and track these components throughout the transfer and hauling process. These integrated technologies adapted from the electronic toll industry, various Intelligent Transportation Systems, ITS and commercial applications can significantly improve freight efficiency and simultaneously security.

These technologies are particularly relevant in seaport operations. Seaport operations utilize tracking and scheduling system at present to match and schedule incoming cargo with arriving trucks. These systems would need to interface with the security systems of tracking and clearance. The security and tracking systems would not replace existing seaport tracking and scheduling systems but would expand their functionality.

As an example of the potential to integrate technologies would be an intermodal pre-clearance system. This system would include technology from the Electronic Toll Collection, ETC industry and might operate as follows. As a vehicle approaches the seaport, an ETC transponder that is used for toll collection is read by an overhead reader. Information on the registry of the vehicle, the individual operating the vehicle and any cargo would be recorded and any port fee or other toll would be collected. To transmit all of this information the technology to identify the individual, the cargo on board and the vehicle would have to be integrated and stored on the OBU. On the same gantry, a laser scan device would classify the vehicle and identify the type of vehicle. Prior to arrival at the seaport, X-ray and ion scanning devices could report any anomalous materials that might be carried on board. Since these devices require a very low speed or no speed condition, a pull off area would be required. All of this information would become immediately available to seaport scheduling and tracking systems. This is much sooner than occurs presently in most configurations where little is known of the vehicle or its cargo until arrival at the port. More timely information would increase the likelihood of being able to match the vehicle to the load and/or be prepared to accept the cargo being delivered.

Security would be improved in several ways. First, better tracking of the vehicle, cargo and operator inherently provides a better level of security. Secondly, RFID cargo tags could maintain data on board concerning electronic seals on containers that ensure unauthorized access to the container had not occurred in transit. Finally, ion and XRAY scanning prior to arrival at the port or upon leaving the port would provide a greater degree of assurance and protection against smuggled materials and explosive devices. Of significant value, is that many of these security functions could be handled off seaport property, allowing for a more efficient use of available seaport space. All of this tracking and security information would be integrated into existing port systems and should significantly improve the operation and functionality of those systems.

Fund Allocation and Efficiency in Transportation

Funding for transportation, and, in particular, highways, is a patchwork quilt with many complications that few understand. This process of funding has evolved from the many layers of statute and bureaucratic processes put in place to allocate federal transportation funds. It is perhaps best defined by the term "categorical funding." This process derives from the allocation funds to specific categories based upon the mode or type of transportation such as rail, bus, or roadway; the program or type of facility, such as interstate highway, primary highway, bus depot or capital for bus purchases; and specific policy program such as a railroad grade crossing. This categorization of federal funding has been in existence since the first gasoline tax was levied in 1916.

At its best, categorical fund allocation is intended to ensure that states carry out programs that inure to the benefit of the public as a nation or accomplish a specific national goal such as the completion of the interstate highway system. At its worse, categorical funding slows the expenditure of funds. Requiring all state projects to comply with eligibility criteria that are defined at the national level, makes the use of federal funds less than optimal and it is difficult to use federal funds efficiently.

Prior to the passage of the Intermodal Surface Transportation Efficiency Act (ISTEA) in 1991, there were approximately 44 categories of funds. The ISTEA legislation attempted to reduce the number of categorical funds and simplify the process. However, the introduction of new summary funds had to be added to the old funds until such time that the accounting for all old funds was complete. The result was a further complication of the categorical funding process but over time the process will simplify. Categorical fund allocation presumes that projects are funded on a cash basis and most federal transportation funds must be matched with state funds before a project can be undertaken. State dollars are then expended on the project and the portion that was budgeted as federal is later reimbursed through a process similar to a billing process. Federal program matching requirements vary by program.

State matching funds can come from general funds such as sales tax, income tax, etc., but in most cases they come from a form of state gasoline tax or other transportation-related tax, such as automobile sales tax. Because regions or transportation districts of a state want to ensure that they receive a fair share of the taxes generated from their area, further allocation processes exist at the state level. State funds are allocated to regions based upon factors such as population, roadway mileage or land area. State revenues must be sufficient to match federal funds for projects and only then can state funds be allocated to other projects. There have been occasions when state revenues have been inadequate to match available federal allocations to the state and federal funds could not be used. Project funding is further complicated by the fact that any given project may be eligible for more than one source of federal funds, each with potentially different matching requirements. Each year state departments of transportation must prepare a new program plan for identifying the allocation of funds to projects. These capital program plans are typically for five years or more and must balance all projected state and federal revenue over the period.

The administration of a transportation program is a complex and difficult process and the organizational resources necessary to manage and account for such procedures is tremendous. State organizations must ensure that federal policy objectives are met or that the distribution of funds is consistent with all federal and state requirements.

In addition to federal funding requirements, states also possess fund categories that have project criteria that must be met before a project can have funds allocated to it. These requirements are the result of state legislative actions and further complicate the process.

Through the process of allocating funds, tracking the expenditure and reimbursement and preparing the annual work program, the focus of producing a final product can be lost. The desire to ensure that each state receives its proper share of federal funds and that regions within the state receive a proper share of their gasoline tax returned diverts attention from the central goal of providing sufficient capacity. In addition, the fund categories that are devised at the federal and state levels to ensure policy objectives are carried out further this diversion of attention.

Organizational Arrangements

The USDOT has the responsibility to oversee the design and construction of transportation facilities paid for with federal funds. This responsibility began with the gasoline tax and the formation of the federal Bureau of Public Roads. Over time an organizational structure has evolved that provides the technical expertise to ensure uniformity and quality in federal transportation projects and to track the appropriate use of federal funds. While the federal structure has gotten smaller in recent years, and more emphasis has been placed on reporting by the states, the USDOT retains a sizeable presence in each state as well as a regional organizational structure. The primary focus of which is to ensure funding conformance and regulation of federal standards for design and construction.

Protection of the environment during the construction of transportation facilities is a critical public agenda and both state and federal agencies are involved in the process. Environmental regulations emanate from state and federal legislation and may require different reporting processes on projects. If environmental reporting processes of the federal and state agencies are reconciled, there is usually a duplicate review of the same material. For large projects that may have significant environmental impact a full environmental impact statement is required and receives a separate review from the state and federal agencies. Even if the requirements of the state environmental process are identical to the federal process, broadly varying approvals can result from separate reviews. Regulatory compliance is fundamentally based on scientific measurement and comparison to a standard however; subjective interpretation of statutes and standards is an inherent factor in environmental review. Efficiency in the design and construction of transportation projects can be particularly affected when the findings of one level of government must be reconciled to those of another. The nature of regulation perhaps precludes the adoption of a single point of approval, but much efficiency could be gained if certification processes are employed that allow one level of government to function on behalf of the other. Because of the sizable capital costs of transportation projects, streamlined organizational processes are particularly relevant to prevent unnecessary delay and increased costs.

Political Agendas

Transportation programs are replete with political agendas. The United States expends $120 billion annually at all levels of government on transportation. The engineering design community, the contracting community, attorneys, investment bankers, labor unions, government employees, environmental activists, commercial developers, the trucking industry, railroads, airlines, and many other influential groups are involved in either the provision of transportation or are significantly effected by transportation projects and programs. Many political action committees exist and represent an enormous source of political campaign contributions. Each of these groups has a vested interest, and in some cases, those interests center on the status quo. At the worst, these politically active interests hinder progressive changes in transportation policy and at the least they ensure that change is incremental. Those who have political ambition must address the interests represented. A major political concern of any politician involved in transportation is ensuring that their constituency receives its share of funding "off the top" of the allocation process.

The people impacted by the decisions made in transportation include the disabled, the elderly, homeowners, minorities, businesses and individual citizens—in short, everyone. With the many powerful interests represented in the transportation industry, it is incumbent upon politicians to protect the interests of the public at large. They must attempt to ensure equity amongst the political jurisdictions, provide for those disenfranchised by the transportation system, and balance the myriad of agendas represented.

Current processes controlling the allocation of dollars, current law regulating the issuance of tax-exempt debt, the process by which construction contracts are awarded, the technical selection of engineering services and many other laws and procedures collectively establish momentum in the transportation process. For meaningful, significant change to occur no portion of the legal/administrative framework of transportation can be "off limits." Full and careful examination of the legal/administrative framework should be a part of any federal reauthorization legislation, and state and local governments should begin the process to do likewise to ensure the most efficient provision of transportation.

5

The future, according to some scientists, will be exactly like the past, only far more expensive.

—John Sladek

POSSIBLE PRESCRIPTIONS FOR IMPROVEMENT

This set of ideas for improving surface transportation systems are not offered as a complete solution accounting for all political, social and economic facets of transportation policy. They are not final conclusions but are offered as a beginning for debate, a "straw man" of possibilities. The complexities of providing transportation facilities are many. It is not however helpful to simply state some of those complexities and end the discussion. Trends and recent events offer a glimpse of possible solutions that should be considered.

Conceptual discussion can only be a beginning. As with other complex policy endeavors, "the devil is in the details" of implementation and policy alteration will require great care to avoid the potential for unintended consequences. However, the data presented earlier on the growing effects of congestion suggest that time is of the essence. If the analysis of congestion based on average national traffic growth is correct, the time has arrived for action and unnecessary delay in beginning the process of change could be devastating to economic competitiveness.

Many solutions could be considered within the realm of "more of the same." One possibility is to double our existing primary source of transportation funding, the gasoline tax, to mirror other developed nations and by doing so, attempt to affect driving behavior. Such an approach might slow the demand for transportation and the growth in traffic experienced over the last forty years. Regardless of whether such a policy could be passed in the legislative process, more gasoline tax does little toward establishing a link between the demand for transportation and the price paid.

Another solution might be to simply cordon off major city centers to highway traffic during certain peak periods. Such solutions have been implemented in other parts of the world but would likely meet with substantial resistance in the U.S. since they would be viewed as limiting basic freedoms. Proposals for change must be realistic and allow for a transition from current practice.

To begin the formulation of potential prescriptions, consider the conclusions offered by the data:

1. There is a close relationship between the highway mode of transport and economic vitality

2. The arterial system of highways carries the majority of commercial traffic

3. There is little connection between the use of transportation and the price charged for that service

4. Congestion is a non-linear function even when traffic growth rate is stabilized at a steady rate

5. There are numerous inefficiencies throughout the transportation funding and development process

These conclusions are particularly appropriate for major highway projects. Schedule delays and funding accumulation through the categorical allocation process can be particularly harmful and cause delays to projects that have a large impact on congestion and therefore the economy.

The federal policies with regard to the interstate system are also crucial to this point. Because the federal congressional and executive leaders have concluded that the interstate system has been completed, very little capital is available for new capacity. The highway system that carries the most traffic, freight and passenger in the urban and rural areas is provided no capital for expansion from the federal level. Considering the costs involved in interstate construction and expansion, it is very difficult for the state to allocate the funds. One interstate project would likely mean the scrapping of dozens of other construction projects across the state. In essence, capital for interstate expansion in the U.S. from traditional sources will not be made available.

Several tools are available to address congestion and improve transportation. Unfortunately, there is a tendency to present partial solutions as a panacea or "silver bullet." To do so merely causes the citizenry to lose confidence in government's ability to deal with transportation issues and lessens the ability to gain broad support of the community. A single solution that will resolve congestion does not exist. There is no "silver bullet" that will resolve all the transportation problems of a nation or region. Comprehensive solutions will be multimodal, apply the best of technology and be politically practical. In the past we have seen transportation planning, technology, intermodalism and various forms of mass transit interpreted, if not presented, as complete solutions to the growing transportation dilemma of congestion. Many eloquent theories have been advanced but there has been little impact on the growing congestion. While these "silver bullets" may be advantageous for political purposes, very little is accomplished towards setting sound long-term transportation policy or affecting congestion.

Incremental or Major Change

To what extent must the process of providing and managing transportation in the U.S. be modified? Will fine-tuning of transportation policy yield the sufficient results or do the issues demand a more fundamental approach? At the heart of such questions is the belief that significant risk does exist for continuing the present course and that it is not a simple matter to modify transportation policy and it will be easily implemented. There will likely be a tendency towards an incremental approach because this will incite less resistance by jurisdictions, politicians and the many vested interests, public and private. However the severity of growing congestion may lead to a more aggressive solution to reverse declining conditions that may have far reaching consequences. Determining the proper scope of transportation policy alteration may be one of the most difficult challenges in creating new solutions. The scope of change must be sufficient to accomplish the primary goals and yet minimize the resistance and it must be politically defensible. The analysis thus far would suggest that a completely incremental approach will not be sufficient. Indeed, our desire to minimize resistance may have resulted in an incremental approach that has led the nation to its current predicament. However, a grand scheme of massive proportions that will have far reaching consequences will likely not gain the political champions it will take to make change a reality.

The theme of this work has been the economic considerations of our transportation systems. Transportation policy cannot however avoid the fact that transportation has a requirement to serve the public at large. It is a public good and to some extent it must be provided to all, guaranteeing a basic minimum of access to the transportation system allowing participation in the economic system and quality of life. To do otherwise would disenfranchise major segments of society. Successful transportation proposals will incorporate a provision of basic transportation for all and providing premium services for those who are willing and able to pay for it. To continue in the assumption that all transportation must remain equally available to all could be an acceptable goal, if we are willing to set taxation levels that will support such policies. However, the politics of raising transportation tax would preclude such an approach. It is highly unlikely, for example, that we will see gasoline taxes of the magnitude in Europe and other parts of the world. Some form of pricing, however, should be applied at all levels of transportation to prevent unconstrained demand. Each of us wants unlimited transportation without an accompanying cost but supporting such views with political rhetoric is not constructive.

The financing of transportation through pricing in some form seems to hold great promise. By altering the financing mechanism changes will naturally occur in related policies and procedures. By reestablishing the fundamental economic equation of supply, demand and price, the invisible hand of the economy and rational economic decision making will alter both supply of transportation and demand for transportation. Such an approach is fundamental to the philosophical premises of our society. A transition to pricing transportation must however include a period of transition. Not all transportation finance should be altered at once and not all highways must be financed in the same manner.

Transitioning from the Gasoline Tax

The surrogate user fee of gasoline tax is well established and the process for collecting and allocating it is equally well established. No matter how large the gasoline tax rate, it will do little to control demand and is inadequate to fund transportation. However, gasoline tax may serve in a new role as a sort of general fund for transportation. Gasoline tax could serve as the funding mechanism for basic transportation access and in time may become a local source of funding for regional transportation systems. The arterial and major highways are the most likely candidates for pricing scenarios. One of the most difficult transportation tasks at the local level has been the establishment of dedicated source of funding for bus and rail operations. A new apportionment of this general transportation tax (gasoline tax) may provide that funding source and is more appropriate than property taxes or other non transportation related taxation. An important part of any new apportionment of gasoline tax should be to fund the non-arterial highway systems. These systems serve a very important public purpose in providing access to the transportation network and must not be left behind in the desire to find a source for transit funding. The arterial system must find a new source of funding that is appropriate to its purpose.

With passage of ISTEA legislation in 1991, the USDOT and the state departments of transportation jointly defined a network of highways that were termed "highways of national significance." This system is composed of the interstate highway system, major urban expressways, and other arterial roadways throughout the United States. Of the 65,000 miles identified the Interstate represents roughly 2/3 with 44,000 miles. The interstate system is only 1.2% of the total public road mileage in the United States, but carries 24% of the traffic and an estimated 80% of the truck freight.[84] Because this arterial system has the most economic impact, it should be the system on which we begin to establish a price for use relationship. We should differentiate between the pricing of passenger cars and commercial traffic, and we should do so with proven technological approaches already available and in operation.

If a pricing relationship is established on the arterial system, it is important to rebate those portions of the gasoline tax that are currently paid for travel on this system. As direct user fees are applied to segments of the arterial system, gasoline taxes should be adjusted and the gasoline tax used on that system returned to the user. This is particularly important for commercial freight movement to prevent double taxation and abnormally higher commodity prices in the short term. Transportation systems will adjust as new direct user fees are applied and the most economical routing and transit are determined. Many technological methods of user fee collection are available for calculating gasoline tax rebate. If the European methods of implementing heavy vehicle direct user fees are followed, especially GPS methods, position data would be available for such a calculation. An option is to allow commercial operators to apply for gasoline tax rebates for miles traveled on toll roads.

Modifying Public Sector Organizations

Consideration of how public sector organizations can "operate like a business," requires some definition. For brevity, let's define private entities as those operating at the highest efficiency to maximize profit (any business) and pubic organizations as those organizations providing public goods and services in an equitable manner to all the citizenry (government agencies). While public organizations are typically responsible for providing public goods, it does not follow that public agencies must own, operate, maintain and/or finance public goods. While the public sector has contracted many activities to the private sector, it is a rarity in the U.S. to allow the private sector full responsibility for operations or to allow the profit motive to drive decision processes. This is, however, precisely the method used on the majority of arterial highway networks in the world. They are provided through the private sector or through joint ventures with the private sector. This is done through the award of concessions to the private sector to build, operate and maintain specific roadways. The contract document protects the public interest and allows the private sector to operate to maximum efficiency within those parameters for a concession period. At the end of that time the project reverts to the ownership of the public agency.

Can public agencies alter the traditions of the public sector and begin to operate more like the private sector? Ideally, public agencies should learn to think like a business, but they must simultaneously realize that they are not one. They must strive to release control rather than holding onto it, keeping only that authority necessary to ensure the public trust is not violated. They must strive to be efficient but ensure equity.

A change in perspective can arise out of education but a fundamental philosophical change must occur in the expectations of those who serve in the public sector. The public sector should begin to view the users of the transportation systems as customers rather than citizens and shift the focus from one of regulation to provision of transportation. Decisions should be made that incorporate the market forces of the economy as well as the desires of the public expressed through elected officials. To an extent, public managers must think and operate as a business. They must understand the public and private attributes of goods and services and understand how those attributes may change with pricing and availability. A greater appreciation of the value of time savings and economic impact should be balanced against the need to regulate and ensure equity. Too great an emphasis should not be given to the priority of ensuring equity and the impact of decisions must be considerate of the long term impacts. A process that fully considers the economic efficiency of decisions in the long term could result in shorter delivery times and a quicker response to congestion.

The balance of the public and private perspectives may be ideal but it should nevertheless be a goal. Perhaps the most influential aspect of the decision process is the issue of averting risk in public management. Risk adversity in the public sector is of paramount importance and more often that not is rewarded in the public personnel process and the degree to which public agency leaders are viewed as successful.

The dilemma of efficiency and equity is demonstrated clearly in the area of public transit. Because of the desire to ensure that everyone has a minimal access to transportation, we have created a system in which both highways and transit are under funded. One might expect that focusing on the economics of transportation decisions would lead to a high level of funding for highways to the detriment of other modes. Such an outcome is conceivable however, in an effort to justify public transit economically; we have developed an elaborate system of fare collection that makes every client of transit keenly aware of the fare while the highway is perceived as being free.

Clearly, our ability to sustain a long-term vibrant transportation system will require that all modes of transportation be funded to adequate levels. Though the highway may most directly affect our economic future, we must consider ways to offer economical incentives to encourage other modes of transportation. The national average for transit operating costs paid from the fare box is thirty percent. Is it an economical decision to collect at all? If public transit is the mode that should be stimulated by policy shouldn't it be the urban passenger mode that is free from pricing?

Another decision process worthy of economic perspective is that of developing intermodal centers, whether passenger or freight. Rather than focus on the vehicles and system network (rail or bus), perhaps a greater focus should be placed on the process of intermodal transfers. Perhaps passenger stations (intermodal centers) should be established that are consistent with a plan for growth and then develop the transit means to "connect the dots." Rather than assuming that seaport operations are predominantly a private activity, perhaps there should be a focus for more efficient freight movement stimulated by the use of public funds and high volume highway spurs developed into seaports. While the term "intermodal" has been inculcated in the planning vernacular since 1991 with the passage of ISTEA, the practicality of funding and operating intermodal centers has just begun to get attention, perhaps because they are at the intersection of public and private interests.

Transportation decision processes must also be appropriate to the jurisdiction. Transportation systems decisions must be made at the appropriate level and not held hostage by local politics. The metropolitan areas of the U.S. are classical examples. Many urban areas have grown beyond established jurisdictional boundaries. New regional urban transportation agencies should be established to provide transportation similar to the regional mobility authorities being established in Texas. Ultimately, these agencies should become multimodal and operate in concert with the state departments of transportation. Such a course is in the economic interests of the region and the nation.

At the core of changing our individual and corporate dependence on the highway is the establishment of a relationship between use and cost in the eyes of the consumer. The same relationship that exists for electrical power, water and other basic services must be established for transportation.

New funding sources are critically important. Rather than depending on the ability of government alone to tax for transportation and the provisions of tax exempt debt to build toll roads, we must find ways to attract private capital by offering competitive rates of return for both start-up and established projects alike. If our task were to develop a self funding mechanism for moving freight from a busy seaport, how might a for-profit intermodal center be funded and constructed that guaranteed movement of goods out of the port within a prescribed time? Several questions immediately come to mind. How much is it worth to the carrier and to the public to get freight out of the port? How much would a carrier be willing to pay to guarantee the movement? Such a scenario might lead to the construction of a separate roadway for freight movement jointly funded by the public and private sectors based upon how much benefit accrues to each. It is possible that private funding could be a major source of capital provided that rates of return are competitive. Most likely such a project would require close cooperation of the public and private sectors and a blending of funding sources.

There are, of course, tasks that the public sector is more properly suited to perform. These tasks require an emphasis on questions of fairness and frequently involve protection of public assets or citizens rights. An example of such tasks might be the acquisition of right-of-way for transportation projects or minimizing transportation project impacts on the environment or society. Such tasks require considerable public input and the establishment of processes that are designed for ensuring fairness and the protection of citizens' rights, not necessarily efficiency. Public organizations should also be responsible for regulating safety and ensuring uniformity. Design standards, sign standards, striping and inspection methods are crucial to preserve public assets and protect the safety and welfare of the traveling public. Private companies should not be placed in the position of having to choose between profitability and stewardship of the public trust.

The Role of the Private Sector

The private sector is more suited by culture, tradition and organizational ethics to be efficient and profitable. Activities that require hiring personnel, acquiring large equipment, and meeting schedules are more efficiently handled by the private sector and driven by economic motives. This is not because private sector personnel are more capable than the public sector, but it is because the private sector is not required to follow public procurement processes or public personnel recruitment standards. Procedures, processes, rules and laws have been formulated to focus the public sector on fairness. The private sector culture of efficiency is appropriate for activities such as maintenance and operations of public transportation facilities. Reducing and controlling costs and applying technology to gain efficiency are tasks well suited to the private sector.

Transportation agencies have historically contracted for design, construction and in recent years have begun contracting for maintenance. Toll operators have begun to contract for manual toll collection and have contracted for design, construction and maintenance. While other nations have established concessions, the concept has been slow to develop in the United States. It is a small step however considering the extent to which maintenance and operations have been privatized. Performance based contracting has become increasingly used to carry out these functions. Rather than contracts that depend upon units of activity, such as acres of grass mowed as a measure of payment, performance based contracts ensure that grass is maintained at a certain height. It is the responsibility of the contractor to maintain that performance through whatever techniques, equipment etc. that he deems appropriate. Performance based contracting will play a central role in the transition from contracting to concessions. It is has been demonstrated to be effective in asset management for maintenance and increasingly for operations.

Applying pricing mechanisms to transportation facilities is another activity well suited to the private sector. Europe, Asia, Australia, and even China have entrusted transportation facility operations to the private sector through a mechanism of concessions. Private sector companies typically are offered concessions for a thirty-year period in exchange for attracting the private capital to design, construct, operate and maintain a facility. At the conclusion of the concession, the facility is turned over to the public. Such arrangements are regulated by the public sector for agreed upon management fees to be charged and standards to be followed. The profitability of such concessions depends upon the financial feasibility of the project and projections of feasibility determine whether the facility is constructed. Risk sharing arrangements between the public and private sector are frequently employed.

Such concession agreements offer the opportunity to attract private capital worldwide. Once a concession has been awarded, there is little opportunity for politics to alter the contractual arrangement without incurring financial penalties. Politics plays little or no role in assessing capital market viability. A project is economically feasible or not; the marketplace determines the ultimate success of the project. The economic decisions of customers to pay a fee for time savings and convenience accumulate to a successful price for use facility.

Most concession arrangements throughout the world are a form of equity financing. Shares are sold in the ownership of the revenue producing transportation facility and may be purchased by the government or by private individuals. Majority ownership varies by project. In the United States priced transportation facilities are almost exclusively funded through a tax exempt municipal debt market. This very efficient system can preclude the construction of facilities that do not demonstrate feasibility to the public markets since bonds must be sold in the marketplace. It would be very difficult to do so if the project is not projected to generate sufficient revenue to pay the principal and interest.

If public funds are used to develop projects that might not be projected to be self sustaining but in the public interest, such projects might be constructed. These public/private partnerships are difficult to conclude because they represent the intersection of public and private thought, perspective, culture and interest.

Establishment of Direct User Fees

It is clear that the history of funding transportation in the United States has led to a focus upon allocation rather than economic efficiency and this allocation of transportation funds serves several key agendas. First, allocation supports the concept of fairness and equity among the states and among the various policy priorities of Congress and the administration. Second, allocation allows for a redistribution of funds to ensure that sufficient funds exist in each state to complete projects of national interest, such as the interstate system. While some of these goals are laudable, the allocation process also spawns organizational growth to support it and moves the policy focus away from project completion and providing necessary transportation infrastructure. The allocation process is synchronous with appropriations and budgeting processes and has led to an assumption of "pay-as-you-go" as the primary financial strategy.

As opposed to analyzing the financial strategies available for developing a project, pay-as-you-go requires the accumulation of funding over time until sufficient dollars are available to solicit contracts to design or construct a project. Such an approach is inherently inefficient because the interest earnings on funds held by the public sector are less than the cost increases experienced for construction or right-of-way acquisition. Also, interest earnings are not always returned to transportation trust funds. When interest earnings are not returned, there is a net loss to the transportation purpose and even if interest earnings are returned, they do not offset inflationary costs. While these considerations may seem incidental, they accumulate over time. This leakage of resources from the transportation purpose and the policy of pay-as-you-go requires funds be spread across many projects through annual appropriations. Delay and higher ultimate costs are the outcomes. While time value of money and the delay that precipitates from annual appropriations and allocation processes significantly affect the financial resources available to transportation, opportunity costs are more relevant to the ultimate economic impact of transportation projects.

Opportunity Costs and Direct User Fees

While perhaps more difficult to understand than inflation costs, opportunity costs can be significantly greater. Imagine a fictional city of 500,000 people that has a broad economic base, including industrial manufacturing and services such as finance and insurance. This hypothetical city has an interstate highway running north and south but is in great need of an expressway east and west and funding from federal and state sources is insufficient to construct the highway.

Imagine now two separate and distinct futures: one where the project is built and one where it is not. If the project is built, additional economic growth and job creation occurs and businesses place a higher market value on existing and newly developed properties. Over a twenty-year period the corridor has a much greater economic value to the community.

If the project is not built, growth will continue but eventually traffic congestion will limit economic enterprise in favor of other locations with a better transportation system. These locations may be in the metropolitan region but they may also be outside the region, state or even the nation. After twenty years the economic growth of the area reaches equilibrium with the transportation system.

Consider the economic variance between the two possible futures. While it may be interesting to attempt to conduct a detailed economic analysis, one can intuitively understand that economic opportunities would have been lost if the project were not constructed. The difference between the economic well-being of these two scenarios represents the opportunity costs.

Research has attempted to quantify opportunity costs that are cumulative to those of congestion delay. Research on congestion delay has established a correlation between delay and economic impact. Those costs have been documented in the work by Weisbrod, Vary and Treyz[85] and demonstrated a 10 per cent reduction in travel time region-wide results in a savings of $1.2 billion annually for the cities of Philadelphia and Chicago alone.

Opportunity costs are those costs incurred when a project is not built and represent the economic gains not realized. Opportunity costs include: the inability to attract industries to the city, the lack of development of companies to support the growing population, the secondary effects of development of business, and other factors. Two attempts have been made to quantify opportunity costs. The city of Melbourne, Australia, performed a study of opportunity costs related to the potential construction of a roadway in Melbourne.[86] The study documented opportunity costs of 16 per cent per year. An annual sixteen percent rate compounded over a thirty year period far exceeds the economic impacts of inflation or congestion delay. Interestingly, opportunity cost analyzes are rarely considered in the decision process to construct a transportation facility. Inflationary and congestion delay are more commonly considered.

Often times a concessionaire will include opportunity cost analyses when preparing projections of traffic for a concession proposal and therefore have a better appreciation of probable traffic. In effect, the concessionaire accounts for traffic generated by growth resulting from the existence of the project. Such an analysis is foreign to most public agencies. The classical approach to projecting traffic on a future roadway is to project the development patterns of the area based on today's transportation system and assign trips to the roadway network. Trip assignments are further impacted by whether a road is tolled or not. If it is a toll road it will receive less of the trips than a competing "free" road. In practice it has been shown that users will accept toll costs if the savings in time are valued as greater than the toll. Most public agencies would probably underestimate the value of a toll road to the regional economy over time and in some cases, underestimate the revenue that might be generated by the toll road.

Other research conducted by the Congressional Budget Office for investments in transportation in the United States reached similar conclusions about opportunity costs.[87] A thorough analysis of the value of new transportation facilities should certainly include opportunity costs in the public policy decision process.

If the costs of delaying or not building needed transportation facilities are close in magnitude, the higher short-term costs of implementing user fees (interest costs, private rates of return, and collection costs) are clearly offset by the costs of not building the facility.

In addition to generating revenue, user fees also serve the purpose of affecting demand for transportation. Some fee structures are set for the exclusive purpose of affecting demand. Experience has shown however, that fee structures may need to be quite high to have the intended effect on demand. One approach is the construction of "express lanes." Express lanes are typically built parallel to existing lanes and are financially feasible because of high congestion levels in the original lanes. Express lanes serve the purpose of generating sufficient revenue to pay for construction in relatively short periods of time, they are also a mechanism for metering demand through price and they also generate more capacity for economic development in the corridor. Express lanes are ultimately financed by those willing to pay for the higher level of service. Such scenarios are only possible through the application of direct user fees.

Direct user fees are most appropriate when certain conditions are met. First and foremost direct user fee facilities should pay for themselves. The chief requirement of a direct user fee project is the ability to finance the project either through equity or through debt. In either case, the project must withstand the rigors of the marketplace.

Another goal of direct user fee projects should be to affect behavior. Direct user fee projects should be designed to charge more for those demanding a higher level of service such as single occupant vehicles and those who want to use the highway in peak periods. Direct user fee projects should also be priced to provide more revenue than needed to retire the debt, fund routine maintenance, and fund operations. In addition to annual fluctuations that require contingency funds, there should be sufficient revenue to seed the construction of additional facilities. In the case of projects funded through equity, sufficient revenue should be available to provide a reasonable rate of return on investment and thereby encourage investment in new projects. If revenue exceeds even these requirements, it could be used for transportation projects that are in the society's interest but not financially feasible otherwise. Uses of revenue for other than the originating project should be done with care and full disclosure to the traveling public that is generating the revenue through the payment of tolls.

Revenue diversion has occurred on several direct user fee operations and the political motivation to do so is enormous. Through revenue diversion large sources of recurring funds can be made available without the necessity to raise taxes and in some cases bonds have been issued in anticipation of future diversions. Great care must be exercised in such instances to avoid the possibility of converting the originating project from a direct user fee project to one that is just another source of general taxation.

Generally, direct user fee projects should be self contained and separated from projects funded from a general tax or surrogate user fees. If direct user fees were used more often to fund new arterial highway construction and maintenance, existing sources of more general taxation such as gasoline tax might be available for transportation projects that do not "pay their own way" but are nevertheless important to the community as a whole. The funds "saved" from the greater use of direct user fees on large arterial projects might be applied to alternative modes of transportation that provide transportation access generally.

Improving Transportation Funding Methods

Any prescription for transportation funding in the United States must clearly include higher funding levels but also efficient use of funds. Several sets of data shows that transportation needs are outstripping the ability of existing transportation resources to construct and maintain facilities and if our economic well being is a primary concern, the arterial highway should be a funding priority. It has been demonstrated that current rates of gasoline tax are inadequate to maintain current highway sufficiency. Additionally, it is unlikely that political support exists to increase gasoline taxes to levels approaching those of other developed countries. Even if this were possible, gasoline tax maintains a pricing system that perpetuates unlimited demand and eventually will decrease in its revenue generating capability. The introduction of hybrid vehicles, the gasohol phenomenon, and the overall striving to increase fleet fuel efficiency will continue to hamper revenue generation through gasoline taxes.

Our transportation funding future must include the use of direct user fees as a funding mechanism for arterial highway capacity development. The users who are most affected economically by congestion and delay will increasingly be willing to pay for the time savings offered by capacity enhancements as congestion increases delay. Those, who are less able or willing to pay, will also experience lower levels of congestion on the existing network, because the new capacity will draw traffic from the existing "free" network.

Technology has made direct user fees an efficient and viable alternative for funding transportation. Electronic toll collection based on radio frequency identification (RFID) has made it possible to pay tolls at highway speed and has made paying for highway use no different than paying for electrical power consumption or water use. New applications technology, such as Global Positioning Satellite (GPS), will make it possible to expand direct user fees. GPS will most likely be used in commercial vehicle applications rather than in private automobiles, and current RFID technology will continue to serve regional automobile travel needs. The higher cost of GPS on-board units ($1,000) versus RFID transponders ($30) and the necessity to protect the privacy of the public will make RFID technology more compatible with the regional electronic toll collection for personal travel, whereas GPS makes it possible to track commercial traffic. New policy alternatives in transportation pricing are made possible by such technology.

Technology allows many different pricing schemes to be implemented but care must be taken that the "pay for use" philosophy is maintained. Because a user fee scheme is technically possible does not inherently ensure that "pay for use" occurs. For example, if a technology existed that automatically charged fees on a per mile basis, larger vehicles would pay the same as motorcycles. Further, a per-mile fee might represent a regressive taxation policy. That is all users, regardless of income would pay the same amount. Large tractor trailer combinations, small urban cars, hybrids vehicles, motorcycles and electric vehicles would pay the same. A number of accepted public policy agenda could be subverted by such approaches.

A frequent complaint of direct user fees is the argument of double taxation, once for gasoline tax and another for tolls. Though it may be financially feasible to rebate gasoline taxes paid, it can be procedurally difficult. If the average fuel efficiency of a modern tractor-trailer combination is 6 miles per gallon and the total gasoline/diesel tax is $.36 per gallon, the per mile gasoline tax would be $.06. If direct user fees were collected on the network of highways defined by USDOT as the Highways of National Significance, commercial vehicles might be allowed to apply for a gasoline tax rebate based on the miles driven as calculated by on board GPS equipment. A similar process for automobiles would be possible based upon records of tolls paid, but could be more easily implemented in the form of a toll discount since the majority of these trips would be on regional networks.

Off the arterial system, fuel taxes would continue as they are today since other roadways generally provide access which is more generally a public purpose. This system of taxation seems appropriate for both passenger cars and commercial vehicles because those highway networks provide access whether the trip purpose is personal or commercial.

An additional facet of using GPS for commercial vehicles is the increases in efficiency that can result. While the primary purpose of GPS in this proposal is the collection of direct user fees, the instantaneous tracking of vehicles in a just-in-time delivery model is a valuable by product and should stimulate better management of fleet operations.

Another facet of improving the transportation funding process is the consideration of time value of money in the transportation program planning process. Projections of construction cost increases and the timing of the flow of funds are important elements in determining whether a five year work program of projects is attainable. While this concept seems fundamental, transportation program development rarely incorporates such calculations. Transportation needs are classically presented as fixed project amounts in specific years and a dollar amount which is projected to flow from gasoline tax five years hence is considered to have the same value as today. Some project costs are known to vary widely, such as the purchase of right of way. Project costs for design, right of way and construction are typically programmed by fiscal year when sufficient cash is expected to be available to pay as the expenditures occur. Even long-term financial planning processes, that extend ten or fifteen years, rarely account for the time value of money. Dollars available in 2020 are assumed to have the same buying power as those available today. At no point are opportunity costs considered.

Construction cost indices must also be continuously monitored and compared to the cost of borrowing in the marketplace. Simply put, the cost of borrowing relative to the cost increases for project expenditures should determine whether it is most financially efficient to borrow or pay-as-you-go. Frequently however, construction cost indices exceed the cost of borrowing and the increased costs of right of way are rarely less than the cost of borrowing. When this is the prevalent condition and funding methods are based on cash in hand, projects expected 4 or 5 years in the future in a capital program may be much longer reaching the construction stage. This is particularly true when attempting to accumulate funds from an allocation/categorical funding process because the available funds are divided amongst so many projects, all of which must be eligible to use the various categories of funds. Under such conditions the use of borrowing should be much more prevalent than is currently the case. However, care must be taken in the borrowing process to assure that revenues will be available to repay the debt and that the process is lowest cost to the public. Perhaps the worst case scenario would be over borrowing against future revenues that don't occur. For example, borrowing against the total anticipated revenue from the gasoline tax would seem inadvisable since the ability to project these revenues long term are affected by many rapidly changing variables.

The transportation funding allocation process is such a predominant factor in planning transportation programs that the time value of money and other standard financial practices are overshadowed. Federal processes require that projects fit a category eligible for reimbursement, and additionally states allocate funds geographically. Various factors of population, area, mileage of highway, etc., are used to make these geographical allocations. Once state allocations are made to regions, local priorities may dictate further project funding adjustments. There is also a tendency to spread highway funding to more projects than necessary in order to placate political agendas. Categorical funding requirements and allocation processes, therefore, result in small amounts being programmed to projects annually and it takes several years to accumulate sufficient funding to let a contract for construction.

The total development time for transportation projects is also affected by the time it takes for a project to move through each step of planning, design, property acquisition and construction. Once partial funds are allocated to a project local priorities may change as reflected through the designated Metropolitan Planning Organization (MPO). Other factors such as varying interpretations of environmental regulations at the federal, state or local levels of government, local opposition or changes in local priorities resulting from changes in local political leadership can also lengthen project development time. Because planning, design, property acquisition, and construction are typically carried out in a linear fashion annual funding cycles may be missed resulting in further delay.

Metropolitan Planning Organizations, MPO are designed to provide a forum for expanded local input and would seem a logical and democratically sound approach. Prior to the broadened mandate prescribed for MPOs in federal ISTEA legislation in 1991, project priority was predominantly set by the state departments of transportation. In practice the effect has introduced further uncertainty in priority and further project delays. Although the priority setting process was envisioned in federal legislation to be a shared responsibility between the state and local governments, MPOs have played a larger role and some state departments of transportation have nearly abdicated responsibility to avoid conflict. Further it is difficult as a public employee to advocate a position on priority that is not accepted by locally elected officials. At its worst, project priority is determined based on local factors rather than the larger state interest.

Because considerable transportation program value can be lost to inflation, financial inefficiencies and opportunity costs, some of the total funding shortfall might be reduced by completing projects more quickly. To demonstrate this potential economic impact, consider the following hypothetical scenario. If inflation is assumed to be 5 per cent and opportunity cost is assumed to be 16 per cent, the annual economic loss resulting from project delay is 21 percent. Also for each year a project is delayed or advanced a compounding effect occurs. If the typical project development time of 12 years could be reduced to 7 years, an economic efficiency occurs. Considering inflation only, this would represent a financial gain of 28 percent compounded annually, not just 25 percent. The value of speeding the project development time is often times overlooked as a real cost to the economy. If borrowing is performed to speed the development time then the economic gain is reduced by the cost of borrowing.

The most significant cost, however, is the opportunity lost for economic growth. At a compounded rate of 16 per cent, the opportunity cost of delaying a project for 5 years is 210 per cent. On a total capital program of $60 billion, a five year improvement in delivery times would be over $120 billion. It is clear from this simplistic analysis that combinations of strategies for reducing project development red tape and advancing projects through carefully planned borrowing should be considered. If the research conducted by the Australians and the USDOT are correct, delays in transportation capital projects are having enormous economic impacts.

Organizational Issues

The current process of maintaining policy control through fund allocation and categorical funding has created a multi-layered organizational and policy infrastructure. Each of these levels represents the potential for delay through legitimate review and approval processes. Government reviews should not be repetitive and present the potential for different results that must then be reconciled through lengthy discussions. Major policy agenda, such as protecting the environment must be carried out thoroughly but also efficiently. Organizations must be constructed and empowered to make decisions at a single point of contact and to transcend jurisdiction where possible. Processes must be designed to allow approvals and decision making at the lowest level on behalf of all agencies through certification and training programs. To the extent that review criteria can not be the same, the review process should at least be performed once.

All agencies involved in the project development process, including the MPO should consider how projects can be expedited to completion. Improvements in cumbersome organizational structures are a potential for significant efficiency gains that can be accomplished in a relatively short time frame. If concepts like demand pricing, variable pricing and high-occupant toll lanes are to be used to generate new revenue streams and reduce congestion through pricing, the existing organization structures must likewise be modified to catalyze successful implementation.

To bring focus to the production process new organizations must be formed. These new organizations should be regional in scope and focused on delivering projects. They should be state agencies by structure that are guided by local leadership through boards appointed predominantly through a statewide appointment process. Such a structure would provide for local input but would be less affected by local jurisdictional interests. These organizations should be able to arrange project funding through borrowing, equity issuance, private debt placement or other means of financing cost-feasible arterial projects. They must be nimble, business-like and accountable to the interests of the region though not controlled by the local politics. Such organizations should be designed narrowly in terms of the types of projects that can be undertaken but broad in the manner in which projects are accomplished. They should be masters of the application of direct user fee concepts for both demand management and revenue generation. Board members should include business interests, the public, elected officials and the state department of transportation.

The mission of such organizations should be centered on improving the mobility of the region through implementation and should adopt projects for development that are consistent with the plans of the regional MPO organizations. These regional mobility organizations should work closely with state departments of transportation to find the best blend of funding and development methodology to bring projects to completion. The goal of regional mobility which supports the region's economic development plans should not be preempted by local parochial interests. The highest priority should be given to projects that link the centers of commerce through the employment of direct user fee methods that ensure long-term revenue generation and demand management.

Organizations of this kind have been in effect in many U.S. states and new permutations are beginning to occur. As urbanization and suburbanization continue, regional implementing organizations will become more necessary. The historical boundaries of cities and counties will increasingly merge into regional and super-regional urban economic areas and existing political jurisdictions will continue to be resistant to any modification that would reduce their control over transportation finance. Regional mobility authorities are beginning to be established in several states and their primary responsibility has been arterial toll high-ways.

Leadership of Quasi-Public Organizations

The leadership of quasi-public organizations is a critical element of their effec-tiveness. Leadership will emanate from the community and be represented on the board while the executive function is staffed from the professional ranks. The organizational design is intended to allow greater flexibility and less bureaucratic control, but the leadership of the organization will determine its success over the long term. Poor decisions, slow decision making, lack of empowerment of staff or attempting to reinvent policy bound organizations in the likeness of traditional structures will yield limited success. Flexibility and empowerment inherently encompass risk and the potential to make mistakes. The more checks, balances, policies and procedures, the less it is necessary to accept risk in decision making. However, such an approach leads to the slow choking of the agencies vitality and ability to act like a business.

Public management safeguards are of course important. There should be pro-visions for audits, management oversight, financial controls, personnel functions, and prescribed procurement processes control the power of appointed board members and public managers. The safeguards not only help to prevent corrup-tion but also help to eliminate favoritism in decision-making. Because there is more latitude, the public trust can be endangered by the temptation to link polit-ical campaign fund raising to the activities of regional mobility agencies. Large sums of money are borrowed and awarded in design, legal and construction con-tracts. While the goal of a new organization should be marked improvements in efficiency compared to a bureaucratic, policy-laden organization, the public trust must be protected as well. The role of public oversight and audits in such organi-zations should be an important initiative.

The executive leaders of these new organizations are accountable to the board that are in turn selected to represent the public. While executive leadership must be politically aware, the primary agenda of the executive should be the delivery of the program. The board should deal with the political and jurisdictional issues. Board members will, of course, be appointed based upon their political activity but they should also be individuals with an interest in the economy of the area.

The organization's staffing should be within the director's purview to support the executive in focusing the organization to the goals set out by the board. He or she should be given the unimpeded authority to select staff, carry out contract procurement and administer both. With such significant decisions to be made such as selection of legal counsel, bond underwriters, design engineers, construction contractors etc. the proper mix of authority between the boards and staff is crucial. To document this relationship an employment contract should contain not just salary, benefits etc., but a statement of the duties which the Board and the executive should perform. Clarity in understanding this relationship is the frequent cause of the failure of various types of organizations. The risk of this balance of authority coming under pressure from outside influences is immense and protections are necessary for both parties to ensure the public agenda is carried out. Large amounts of money are involved in public works contracting and finance and the potential exists for difficulties.

Executive leadership for local regional agencies has typically been provided from amongst the professional ranks. However, in recent years there seems to be a tendency towards the selection of individuals with significant political histories. Perhaps a greater emphasis is beginning to be placed on the political aspects of decision making rather than the technical. A persuasive argument could be made in either direction but the skills mix between the executive staff and the Board are crucial. Many have advocated that these agencies be established within the state departments of transportation to eliminate this concern. However, while that may lead to a more professional staff selection it could render the regional mobility agency a mere division of the state DOT without the nimble, dynamic charter envisioned.

The board of these regional agencies is typically appointed or defined in statute to represent those constituencies most directly affected by the agency's goals. If the agency's primary purpose is expressway construction on a regional basis, it should have representation from the local elected community and also from the business community. A representative of the state Department of Transportation should also be included. To the extent that an organization is statewide in its purpose, the chief executive of the DOT should be a member of the board. It is imperative that these organizations are extensions of the state transportation department's purpose, not exclusive to the department's purpose. It is the close relationship between the two organizations that provides the financial and political leverage to amplify the capabilities of the regional agencies.

Corridor Preservation

One of the more disconcerting tasks of government is to purchase private property for the construction of a transportation facility. Land ownership and the freedom to use property are fundamental rights guaranteed under the United States Constitution. In contrast to this individual right is the need to purchase right-of-way for the public purpose of constructing transportation facilities. The process is a delicate balance of conflicting values and can be a significant portion of the total project cost, especially in urban areas. The process begins with attempts to reach a mutually agreeable negotiated purchase price. In those cases where accommodation is not possible, transportation agencies have the right of "eminent domain" to acquire the property and use the court system to resolve the value of the purchase plus any "damages" to the property that is not purchased.

The process of transportation project development must consider the costs of acquiring right of way, the costs to mitigate for environmental protection and preservation and the costs to design and build the project. Accordingly, many years of public meetings on various alternative routes precede the purchase of right-of-way corridors. Though some existing residential properties can be affected negatively, the construction of transportation projects usually increases the value of surrounding property.

Land values increase as the project becomes more certain and the specific alignment becomes more definite. Much is at stake for the surrounding land owners and those who would develop the property and great care must be taken during this activity to ensure the public is properly represented. Clearly, the legal rights of the property owner must be protected. Because the process is based upon estimated values of property, it is inherently subjective and the cost of right of way is very difficult to estimate. Many times urban right of way costs constitute a large percentage of the total cost of the project.

While individual rights must be preserved and courts have determined that right-of-way cannot be set aside without compensation to the owner, an alternative is the advance purchase of right-of-way. Today the use of federal funds on transportation projects require that all design work be completed before the purchase of right of way can proceed. While this may ensure that no property is purchased that later design changes may render unnecessary, it also lengthens the project development process and can drive up the costs of right of way. Advance right-of-way purchase is a tool that can reduce costs and remove uncertainty for those landowners willing to sell. While this process may not be appropriate in all cases, projects in urban areas are the most likely candidates where existing or future development may be affected by the construction of a transportation project. Funding for such advance purchases does not necessarily require cash on hand. For example, there may be cases where exchanges of property are in the interests of both the transportation agency and the property owner and this can serve to reduce costs.

Bond issues for the purpose of advance right of way purchase make sense when the cost increases for right of way exceed the cost of borrowing. This approach has been used by some transportation agencies. Additionally, if transportation projects are developed by private concessionaires, it may be possible for a property owner to negotiate an equity ownership in the final product. While this scenario is one not frequently used in the development of transportation projects, the possibility exists and under the right circumstances may be useful.

The process of advance right of way purchase is dependent upon the process used to design a project. Typically, corridors are developed as part of the preliminary design and environmental study process and are very broad sometimes exceeding a mile in width. Studies of the environmental and societal impacts result in potential alignments within these corridors and meetings with the public and further detail studies of impact result in final alignment. During corridor studies it is logistically possible to begin the negotiation process with land owners and occasionally this information will help in finalizing the alignment, but this is not typically done. To the contrary, federal processes require the completion of final design before the right of way acquisition process can begin. The final design incorporates selection of a final alignment and puts the acquiring agency in a weaker bargaining position. With the completion of each step in the development process, there is increased certainty that a project will be built and specifically where the project will be built. Retaining flexibility is a commonly identifying characteristic of an agency attempting to operate as a business and optimizing efficiency.

Business and Technological Context of Direct User Pricing

Clearly transportation in the United States is defined by the ubiquitous automobile and increasingly, the same is true for freight movement by truck. Today, 90 per cent of total freight value travels over the roadway system.[88] To generate acceptable transportation funding that can accomplish the transportation goals necessary to remain economically competitive, we must establish a direct relationship between use and cost for the automobile and truck freight. How do we accomplish such a task?

The fundamental definition of transportation as a public good may provide a starting point. If transportation is a public good as defined by Buchanan[89], are there approaches to pricing public goods that would allow transportation departments or authorities to operate as a business? The hypothetical example of the swimming pool that changes in nature from a very private good to a very public good through pricing demonstrates how public choice behavior might be employed. Remember that when the swimming pool use was governed by a private club and large initiation and monthly fees are charged, few could afford to use the facility. There was also little congestion and an excess supply of the good was present. In the same manner, a transportation facility with very high toll rates would likely have little congestion and would begin to exhibit the characteristics of a private good. It is rare that a transportation facility is priced at such high levels since it is also in the interests of the community to have reasonable access to the facility. The pricing for a transportation project should be priced to "optimize" the use of the facility rather than to "maximize" the profits.

As the pricing of the facility is reduced, similar to the swimming pool example, a transportation facility can change in character from a private facility to a public one depending on pricing. Market forces will drive the pricing process according to the value perceived by the customer. To the extent that there is a savings in time, the facility has value and the market will determine the value of the facility if the price is allowed to vary with use. The concept of congestion pricing is based on these market forces.

When only business factors are considered in setting a price, it will be set to maximize profit because that is the interest and purpose of a private firm. In contrast, a purely public consideration would dictate that the facility be as accessible to as many as possible and therefore the pricing would be minimal. The primary concern is equity and availability. A balance between these two perspectives is essential and public officials and the public itself must have a place at the table. Concession arrangements allow a private company to construct what would otherwise be a public facility and price the facility. It is essential that a reasonable and previously negotiated profit margin be set through a process that is reasonably transparent. Care must be exercised by those representing the public that the pricing process continues to demonstrate the attributes of a public good and that there are provisions for public input on pricing. At the end of the concession the project is the property of the public.

Some public agencies operate in a similar manner to concessions and price facilities to return costs and a marginal profit that allows for expansion or extension of capacity. While the tendency for concessionaires is to price to maximize profit, public agencies tend to price for access and equity. Many public agencies are resistant to increasing tolls to a level that decreases demand. Some have even resisted increasing tolls to account for inflation. If public agencies are to affect demand through pricing or generate sufficient funds to expand and improve their arterial networks, they must price the facility accordingly. If this is not done, it is likely that concession arrangements will become more prevalent.

Pricing a public good provides the ability to affect behavior, economically meter use for the benefit of society overall and generate a revenue stream that can be used to further develop the transportation system. To do otherwise is to make the swimming pool free and accessible to all resulting in over use and insufficient capacity. Under such policies it is a self fulfilling prophecy that insufficient capacity will be the result and "we can not build our way out."

Public goods, in the form of transportation do not, always have to be provided by governmental organizations in the United States. Such is not the case in the rest of the world for major roadways. The United States is the anomaly in this regard. Most of the major European roadways are toll roads, funded through joint ventures between government and the private sector or wholly owned for a concession period by a private company. South Africa's National Roads Agency, a quasi-private organization operates approximately 15,000 kilometers of major roadway of which 5600 kilometers are tolled. Thousands of kilometers of motorway are under concession agreements in Europe, South America, and Asia. This is the predominant method by which major roadways are constructed throughout the world and construction is proceeding at an increasing rate.

Concessions offer the opportunity to price public goods and incentivize efficiency through private sector business operations. We are accustomed to such pricing mechanisms for water, sewage treatment, electricity and other essentials to modern living. Regulated utilities, private businesses, commonly provide these goods and this has been the case for many years. This is very similar to roadway concessions common throughout the world. In both cases, price is set to recover costs and a negotiated profit margin.

The congestion pricing project recently implemented in London, England is unique in this regard since the purpose is not to generate revenue but to reduce congestion in the city center. The "Citywide Congestion Pricing" policy requires anyone entering the city to pay a fee. The concept is to reduce congestion in the city for the greater good of all. Peak-period congestion delays have declined 30 per cent since the pricing mechanism went into place in February, 2003.[90]

Prior to the introduction of electronic toll collection, frequently altering price was a difficult and limited proposition. With electronic toll collection, however, charges can be altered for time of day, high periods of congestion, on a per-mile basis and by specific routing. Previous manual collection processes limited the precision with which prices could be changed. With electronic collection methods, tolls can be changed at a moments notice and can be charged to the nearest penny. There are very few limitations on the technical ability to alter rates.

The motivations of the public and private sectors must be kept in mind. The private sector is motivated by efficiency and profit while the public sector is interested in equity and ensuring social justice,[91] similar to that defined by John Rawls as the "protection of the minimum." If a toll road were operated for profit without any governmental controls rates would be set in a manner that could be detrimental to the public need for mobility. Alternatively, if this same toll road were run by a governmental unit, the goal would be to ensure that as many of the citizenry as possible could afford to use the system and as soon as possible to remove the tolls and make the facility free of charge. This approach is also not in the interest of the public need for mobility.

The practical application of public concessions is somewhere in the middle, between the public and private sectors. Other countries have established pricing schemes that optimize the benefit, ensure sufficient profit to continue maintenance, and provide for the accumulation of capital to provide for system improvements and expansion of the network. Throughout the U.S. transportation industry, there is a growing realization that all of these objectives can be met and that pricing mechanisms can act to economically meter demand from the unconstrained condition of "free" roads.

Internationally there is a growing interest in using pricing to affect demand and in some cases it is the primary goal rather than revenue generation. Many examples of demand management exist throughout the world but the industry in America and the political decision maker are just becoming aware of the possibilities. The London congestion pricing project is an example of just such an approach, but why is this phenomenon happening only now?

Tolls or direct user fees have been documented to the 4th century B.C. in ancient texts such as the Arthasastra in India and in the English Domesday Book of 1095.[92] In the United States the first toll road was Virginia's Little River Turnpike, which stretched 100 kilometers from Alexandria to the Blue Ridge Mountains.[93] In the 1820s Britain had 40,000 km of toll roads operated by over a thousand companies.[94] Toll roads are not a new idea. However, technology in the twentieth century has dramatically changed the concept. The necessity to stop to pay has always been a condition of using a toll road. Had that not been the case, the use of surrogate user fees, such as gasoline tax, may never have happened.

The revolution in toll payment has been the introduction of radio frequency identification devices (RFID) and, more recently, global positioning satellite technology (GPS) that allow for the collection of direct user fees non-stop. While many of the established toll road systems have adapted their facilities to use electronic collection methods, they seem socially and politically bound to the acceptance of cash, as well. Newer roads are being built where the patterns of using cash have not been established and those roads are operating as totally electronic systems. Even newer technologies are being developed that are capable of collecting tolls without on board units.

These technologies have created a paradigm shift in direct user fee processing. Toll operators now know who their customers are. They have access to their customer's mailing addresses, telephone numbers and financial information. With this new access to customers comes the responsibility to treat their information as customer information rather than public information. The assumption that all information is public because the operating entity is a public agency, has ceased with changes in the nature of the project, the public/private characteristics of the operating agency and the voluntary nature of customer use.

While the stop-and-pay toll procedure may not have been an issue in the past, in today's high-volume, high-speed environment it is a great hindrance. The elimination of toll gates has been an issue of great concern and debate because the agency must ensure complete collection and yet the customer wants more convenience and speed. Obviously, if the toll gate is removed, the toll plaza has a greater capacity. However, the toll gate, which is an ancient development of the stop-and-pay era, has been the device to ensure that no one is allowed to pass without paying.

Technology has also altered the cost equation for charging direct user fees. Costs for collecting direct user fees have been wide ranging using a traditional manual approach. The primary cost of collection is labor. Staffing for 24 hours 365 days a year is very expensive and the process of handling cash and accounting for collections requires multiple counts and supervision at each step in the process. Although coin machines of various types have been used to reduce these costs especially in non-peak hours, these devices typically cost $30,000 to $60,000. They require frequent maintenance, removal of debris placed in the basket, resetting for coin jams that can result from poor coin condition or foreign coins and coin machines can be pilfered.

The cost to collect one dollar of tolls varies depending upon the periods of staffing levels and the traffic flow but the average cost to manually collect a dollar of tolls has been about 21 cents in the United States.[95] Modern electronic toll collection has changed this and estimates are between 6 cents and 8 cents per dollar collected. This dramatic reduction in costs occurs only when the percentage of traffic using the electronic system is very high, in the 60 to 80 percent range. The collection costs for all-electronic toll collection systems show promise to even lower, especially for new roadways where the roadways and toll facilities can be designed accordingly. Several all-electronic toll roads operate in the world today; in Australia, South America, Israel, Canada, and most recently in the United States.

Technological developments in toll collection have also changed the comparative collection costs of direct user fees and gasoline taxes. The cost to collect gasoline taxes is not zero. The collection process requires inventory tracking, collections audits and investigation of potential violations. While most states collect such taxes at the wholesale level rather than the retail level, the cost to collect and regulate payment is still approximately 6 percent of the total collected.[96] This covers the cost of collecting, recording, auditing, banking and transferring funds to the appropriate government account.

Interestingly, modern technology can reduce the cost to collect direct user fees to nearly the same 6% level. Additionally, technology has removed the concerns of congestion and labor costs resulting from stopping and paying tolls. Another concern has historically been the issue of double taxation, once for gasoline tax and again for the direct user fee.

The average gasoline tax on a per mile basis in the United States is about 1½ cents per mile based upon a total of 36 cents per gallon and a CAFÉ standard of approximately 25 miles per gallon. The average U.S. urban toll road charges about 10 cents per mile and typically gives a 10 per cent discount for the use of an electronic toll collection device. Some discounts are as much as 50%. Therefore although most are not aware of it, the typical urban toll road is refunding nearly the equivalent of the gasoline tax to the electronic customer. The discount was established to encourage customers to purchase electronic transponders or to encourage frequent use of the toll road system. The unintended consequence of discounts for paying electronically is the refunding of equivalent gasoline tax on a per mile basis.

Technology has removed many of the inconveniences and concerns of applying direct user fees and various methods for pricing transportation are in operation in the United States today. The opportunity has arrived when direct user fees can be based on a range of criteria to affect transportation choice, affect congestion and generate revenue based on various characteristics and do so efficiently. Such pricing opportunities would not be possible in a manual collection environment.

Technology presents some new challenges, however. One of the most significant of these is privacy. Technology can provide information about a person's location, the time of day, and the vehicle being driven. In addition, a range of information is necessary to originate an account: an address, credit card information, driver's license number and other personal information. It is critical that any technological toll collection application protect customer information from unauthorized access and that the records are considered customer records rather than public records. Even though this information is controlled in a secure manner it is also essential to convince the public that this is the case.

To charge a direct user fee, only three pieces of data are required: vehicle identification, location of the vehicle and toll rate. As described, RFID transponders can be used to accomplish this, but other technologies potentially could accomplish the same thing. Cellular telephones are capable of determining approximate location through a process of triangulation, and global positioning satellite equipment is capable of tracking a vehicles location to a great degree of accuracy.

The application of GPS technology creates another level of concern for privacy advocates. In addition to charging tolls, GPS applications inherently identify location. Understandably the public is concerned about the ability to track a personal vehicle. The concerns over privacy in the freight industry are however profoundly different. The ability to track a vehicle in the freight industry is an asset. The person operating the tractor is either an owner/operator pulling a trailer owned by a freight company or is hired by the owner of a fleet of tractors. In either case, there are powerful business reasons to know the exact location of the freight unit. This is especially true in an environment of just-in-time inventory control. The value of location information in logistics management far outweighs the issue of privacy for a freight operator. Because of the added value that location information provides to freight operators, GPS technology seems more appropriate for commercial freight vehicles. The cost of on board units, OBU are also a factor in the choice of technology for personal vehicles versus freight operations. OBUs for GPS applications currently cost about $1000 including installation, whereas the transponders used for RFID electronic toll collection applications are $25 to $30. The higher cost of the GPS units might make since for a commercial vehicle but makes little sense for a personal vehicle even if the privacy concerns were not so prevalent for personal vehicles.

Technology offers many opportunities but solutions must fit the political and economic realities of the state or region in which it is applied. Technological solutions are frequently applied to a portion of a roadway network but technology applications should be considered in the context of the entire regional network. Regardless of the public or private nature of roadway ownership or the manner in which the electronic toll collection process occurs, all segments are part of an intersecting network which serves the public purpose. Standards should be developed for each regional area to accommodate RFID based systems and a national standard should be developed for GPS commercial freight and other frequent interstate travel.

Inadequacy of the Gasoline Tax

The first use of gasoline tax in America was in 1916. This tax of 2 cents per gallon was established to get vehicles "out of the mud." At the time it represented 11 per cent of the price of a gallon of gasoline which was 18 cents.[97] It represented the best surrogate for a user fee that was technologically available at the time and attempted to establish a relationship between use and fee. The majority of the revenue generated was for construction of new facilities; today only about half of the revenue generated by gasoline tax is used for capital construction. As the system grew the requirements for maintenance and improvements grew proportionally and the costs of developing a project increased as well. Expenditures for design, right of way acquisition and construction increased and greater portions of the tax were used for important public agendas other than highways.

Considering the price of gasoline of about $2.00 currently and the federal gasoline tax of 18.4 cents, federal gas tax is 9 per cent of the current price of gasoline. If the average state tax of $.21 is included, the total percentage of the price of gasoline that is represented by tax is 19.7 per cent. On the surface it would seem that the amount paid for gasoline tax is reasonable and should be adequate since the tax appears to have kept pace with the price of gasoline.

Gasoline taxes however have not kept pace with the need for transportation funding. Several measures of use versus price are indicative. When measured against vehicle miles traveled, number of registered drivers or registered vehicles; gasoline tax revenues have been insufficient to keep pace with use. This is not a surprising result considering that there is no perceived connection between price and use. From 1960 to 2000 the miles of roadway in the U.S. increased from 3,545,693 to 3,936,229 or 11%. In the same time, the total vehicle miles traveled on U.S. highways increased from 718 billion to 2 trillion 749 billion, an increase of 282%[98]. Clearly the additions to the highway system have not kept pace with the use.

More recent developments in the United States further complicate the use of gas tax as a stable source of transportation funding. Several events have converged to affect future funding from gasoline tax. Long-term concerns exist about highly efficient hybrid engine vehicles. While they are not a large part of the total vehicle fleet and probably will not be for several years their popularity will grow as the price of gasoline rises. Beyond a ten-year time frame, all electric vehicles and hydrogen vehicles may begin to come into the fleet. There are however much more immediate concerns for the adequacy of transportation funding based upon the gasoline tax.

While hybrid vehicles exist and others loom on the horizon, America has been on a binge for larger vehicles. In the decade of the nineties, the fleet of two-axle vehicles has remained relatively flat representing 133,700,496 vehicles in 1990 and 133,621,420 in 2000.[99] In the same period the number of other single unit two axle four-tire units went from 48,274,555 in 1990 to 79,084,979 in 2000.[100] This latter number represents the growth in vans and sport utility vehicles. Generally these vehicles are less fuel efficient (21 mpg versus 28 mpg for passenger cars[101]) and this has produced slightly more gasoline tax per unit of use and alleviated some of the transportation revenue shortfall. In fact, the average fuel efficiency in 2001 model year was 20.4 mpg, the lowest in two decades.[102]

With exception of nitrous oxides these vehicles are 30-50% more polluting than passenger automobiles.[103] In 2002 the emission standards for automobiles began to be applied to sport utility vehicles and larger two axle vehicles. If the trend towards larger vehicles slows because of tax incentives or the influence of higher gasoline prices, the revenues generated by gasoline tax will reduce at a faster pace.

There are also short-term effects on federal gasoline tax revenues resulting from regulation and the actions of Congress. The latter center on the Revenue Aligned Budget Authority (RABA) established during the last reauthorization in 1997. The intent was to more closely synchronize the expenditure of funds with the flow of gasoline tax revenues and resulted in higher levels of expenditure authorization from 1997 to 2002. Congress was the faced with lower gasoline tax revenue projections and the RABA provisions required an adjustment in the negative. This congressional action is indicative of the desire to increase transportation spending without increasing the level of taxation. Such actions are temporary in nature and do not address the fundamental issue of sufficient transportation funding. Similar philosophies appeared at work during the most recent reauthorization process. Donor states were insisting on a greater return and donor states insisted on no losses in revenue. The solution was to attempt to appropriate more than was projected to be available.

Perhaps more significant than the budgetary issues are the unintended consequences of air quality regulations on transportation revenue generation. One of the primary polluting sources in major urban areas is the personal vehicle. While there are many sources and there have been enormous improvements in reducing automobile emissions, the personal vehicle remains a major source. With modern equipment such as the catalytic converter, the automobile has become much less of a factor in damaging air quality when measured on a per vehicle basis. However, from 1970 to present, the vehicle miles traveled have double leaving a modest improvement overall from vehicular sources, except for lead which has been reduced by 95%.[104] However, carbon monoxide levels reduced significantly from 1983 to 1992 even though vehicle miles of travel increased 35% over that period[105]. Besides the need to find a less polluting fuel source, gasoline tax exemption on the federal level for the use of ethanol will also reduce total collections. As the urban air quality standards have been tightened, more non-attainment areas will likely result and gasohol will more often be introduced as an oxidizing agent. The result will be lower levels of revenue available for transportation.

When added to the pressure to increase fleet fuel efficiency, the introduction of hybrid vehicles with higher efficiency and downward adjustments in authorization of expenditures, the future for gasoline tax as a stable source of transportation revenue seems unlikely.

Besides being a poor surrogate for direct user fees, gasoline tax does not link price with use. As an alternative strategy we could continue to encourage the sale of larger personal vehicles which are more polluting and less fuel efficient but that would certainly be a poor choice from many policy perspectives.

While it may not be possible to replace gasoline tax as a funding mechanism completely in the near term, the possibility exists in the long term. If all new vehicles were equipped with RFID transponders, those vehicles would be able to pay electronically. After a turn over period of 10-12 years nearly all vehicles would be so equipped. In the near term however, it is more likely that electronic revenue collection will occur primarily on major arterial roadways only and gasoline tax and surrogate means of user fee pricing will be used to fund highways not on the arterial system. Regardless of the means of collection, it is clear that the time has come for considering other methods of collecting transportation revenue sufficient to expand major economic corridors to meet demand. Pricing mechanisms will also serve to reduce the demand in those corridors.

Some have advocated a complete replacement of the gasoline tax. Such an approach would likely be disruptive, counter productive to valuable policy agendas and perhaps less efficient than current practice. Just as one size does not fit all, a solution for an urban area will most likely be quite different from one in a rural area. Likewise solutions for freight movement will most likely vary from those we might incorporate for ground passenger service. We must consider the inherent differences of these four unique transportation environs and the associated externalities.

A Prescription for Urban Passenger Travel

Urban passenger traffic is predominantly composed of trips generated by automobiles and light duty trucks (SUVs and vans) and travel in urban areas of the United States has altered with the growth of suburban areas and changes in demographics. With continued suburbanization more trips are taking place between suburbs and within suburbs. Coincidentally the purpose of travel has been increasingly recreational, education related, shopping, etc., and less dominated by travel to and from work. The highway component most related to economic vitality in this setting is the arterial highway and in particular, those highways of high capacity with minimal stops. These same highways serve as the connectivity between suburban centers, universities, airports and the central business districts.

These arterial highways are typically limited access or restricted controlled access highways, carry trips over 5 miles in length and are predominantly the urban interstates and expressways. These facilities were identified as critical to the national interests in the 1991 federal legislation, ISTEA and were titled "Highway of National Significance." While this designation included highways outside urban areas, it includes the urban arterials. They are critical to urban passenger travel, urban freight movement, and freight traffic passing through an urban area. These highways are like the arteries of the human heart that move the vital nutrients and oxygen throughout the body. If congestion occurs in the arteries of the body, eventually a heart attack will result. Like the human body congestion on urban highways will eventually result in an economic heart attack. Traffic growth and limited additional capacity make the ultimate result a certainty, the only question is when it will occur. Political half measures or "silver bullets" may extend beyond an election cycle but they will not address the fundamental issue of congestion.

Highways included in the designation "Highways of National Significance" include two basic classes of highway from in terms of capacity: limited-access and controlled-access highways. Limited-access highways are interstate design highways that are two lanes in each direction and designed for nonstop flow. The maximum capacity for limited access highways is approximately 2,200 vehicles per lane per hour. If interchanges are spaced appropriately, limited-access highways are capable of accommodating the major flow of traffic. In contrast, controlled-access highways are classified by the frequency of curb cuts, left turn lanes and signalized intersections allowed for business or other access. The more frequent the access allowed the more capacity is affected. As access to the highway grows over time, more traffic lights appear and the throughput of the highway is reduced. At best, controlled-access highways can provide capacities of one-half the freeway or 1,100 vehicles per lane per hour. The typical controlled-access highway provides capacity in the 700-800 VPH range or one-third the capacity of a limited access highway. As development occurs the capacity of these highways is further reduced.

Controlling access to a highway is a very difficult task. As the highway matures the development around the highway continues and it is increasingly difficult deny access as a public agency. While these processes are typically regulated through statute and administrative rule, politics can affect a subjective judgment of traffic impact and there is a tendency over time for political pressure to mount for allowing access to the highway. As access is granted via this incremental process, throughput capacity is reduced.

Limited access highways do not suffer the same degree of access controversy. Additional interchanges are frequently requested on limited access facilities but they are predominantly part of the interstate highway system and the federal government regulates the frequency of interchanges specifically to maintain the throughput or interstate capacity. While overall capacity is an important consideration, peak-hour capacity in the urban area is particularly crucial.

Many urban trips tend to take place in the morning and evening peak hours and throughout the work day. These facilities offer an excellent opportunity to begin establishing the price-use connection and this has occurred through the use of high occupant toll lanes, variable pricing, congestion pricing etc.

High occupant toll lanes or HOT lanes sell excess capacity in special lanes that where reserved for automobiles carrying more than one person or buses. They serve the toll payer with faster, premium service while still serving the vehicle carrying more than one person at no additional cost. HOT lanes also reduce congestion in the parallel "free" lanes since some of those who would have used the "free" lanes choose to pay in the HOT lanes.

Variable pricing is a technique for pricing based upon the level of congestion; the higher the congestion on the highway at a point in time, the higher the toll. The intention is to move some of the traffic out of the peak hours of operation and into less congested travel periods. Congestion pricing is basically variable pricing but at a specified time during the day.

Recently, however, congestion pricing has taken a new form, that of behavioral pricing. It is the application of a toll for the purpose of rewarding a certain behavior. For example, the city of London charges for driving past an imaginary line into the London business district during specified periods of the day. The primary goal was to reduce congestion levels in London, as it has done, and secondarily to generate funds. The funds generated are then used for the construction and operations of alternative modes of transportation. This pricing scenario has been devised to specifically alter the preference for driving the automobile into the city center.

Whatever the form of pricing it is essential to be clear on the objectives of pricing. Pricing can be used to affect transit behavior, to generate revenue to build facilities, to optimize the use of a facility, to generate revenue to build alternative transportation modes, to generate revenue to pay the operations cost of an alternative mode, and to pay the cost of maintaining and operating the priced facility. Care must be exercised to ensure that the public agenda is not hijacked for political expediency. George Bernard Shaw once said, "A government that consistently robs Peter to pay Paul, can always count on the support of Paul."

At the very least, these pricing mechanisms are, in essence, metering the availability of a public good through price. From an economic perspective adequate capacity must be ensured and all urban arterials essential to the flow of commerce should be priced. The specific method of pricing and the technological methods used will vary, but from an economic perspective, the core of this strategy must be the ability to generate a revenue stream for funding additional transportation capacity. A key attribute of this revenue stream is that it is dedicated by design to a specific purpose and by so doing avoids the issue of incremental decision making endemic to the allocation of categorical funds.

To prevent the revenue stream from being diverted to a purpose other than regional, provisions must be made to ensure that money accumulated for urban arterials in a given region must stay in that region. While regional authorities will limited financial success have few clamoring to control the revenue stream, those with a significant revenue stream become attractive to powerful local and super-regional interests. The purpose of the entity should also be carefully crafted and changed only with the support of those in the regional community it serves. If the purpose is to fund the urban arterial system, it should not be easily changed nor altered without significant public review. Those who use such a system should have a large voice in the use of funds since it is their use of the system that has produced the revenue stream. Maintenance and additional capacity of the arterial system should be prominent in such considerations to ensure the economic needs of the region are supported. Priced urban arterials also would avoid the unlimited demand dilemma that we find ourselves in today.

Care must be exercised in allowing a concessionaire to develop a complete network of urban arterials as the economic well being of the community is then embodied in the provisions of the concession agreement. If this is to be the case, the leaders of the regional community should have a significant role in the determination of those provisions. A balance must be struck between the profits extracted under such agreements and the long term interests of the region to continue to expand the urban arterial network.

A Prescription for Urban Freight Mobility

Pricing mechanisms have an application to urban freight movement as well as the urban passenger environment. As arterial urban highways are priced, congestion is reduced and urban freight mobility is improved. The value of reducing congestion for the freight industry has been quantified on several occasions.

There is a cost for delay for any vehicle but delay costs for freight movement can be extremely high. For the tractor-trailer, the cost has been documented to be $1 per minute of delay and considering the low margin on truck freight movement, the entire profit for a trip could be quickly eliminated.[106]

Many urban centers are located at strategic geographical centers for transportation and as such are near seaports, inland waterways, rail centers, intersections of major interstate highways and major airports. Urban centers are therefore centers for freight movement and points of freight transfer and warehousing operations. Depending upon the logistics and the unique characteristics of the transportation network, there may exist opportunities for truck-only tunnels, bridges and roadways. Such facilities might be funded by users through pricing and could be operated with the sole intention to move freight. In such a scenario weight limits might be set at a higher level and highways could be designed to handle heavier and longer loads thereby improving the efficiency of freight movement between transfer points such as seaports and warehousing operations in the metro area. Highways for trucks only could be built that would allow very large and heavy loads. Once the loads are transported to intermodal centers or warehouse operations, cargo could be divided into loads acceptable for the public highway system.

Urban freight mobility would also be served by providing for more efficient cargo handling and security clearance. Just as the global community must deal with the issues of safely transporting increasing volumes of freight, the same is true in the urban environment.

Security has become a major concern in freight movement. Technologically it is possible to secure a container and track movement around the globe and record any event when the container was opened. All security activities don't necessarily have to occur at the international port. If intermodal freight centers were designated and secure truck-only facilities or rail facilities were built between the major freight arrival locations and the intermodal center, freight handling efficiency would improve and security could be ensured. The intermodal center could become the center for security and freight transfer.

The Alameda Corridor project is one such concept. The project was designed to improve transportation by removing the at-grade intersection conflicts between highway traffic and rail freight movement. An innovative approach was taken to construct a grade separated rail corridor of high capacity and transfer freight from the seaports to an intermodal freight center. The rail line is for the singular purpose of transferring freight from the seaport to the intermodal center and back. The development of the project eliminated 200 rail crossings and reduced delay on the roadway network by 15,00 hours per day[107]. The goal was to relieve congestion of the highway network in the urban area, increase freight movement capacity, improve security and improve scheduling efficiency at two of the major ports in the U.S. The project has been a phenomenal success and is an example of a freight only connection in an urban area. The same could be done for truck traffic with dedicated highways between seaports and freight intermodal centers built to handle larger and heavier loads.

Separating urban freight traffic from urban passenger traffic is a factor in safety and capacity for both transportation modes. Other than bulk goods, the majority of freight delivery is by truck. Within the urban area, much of the freight activity is in the category of industrial production, distribution or service delivery. Depending upon the economic activity in the urban area, the distribution activity may be long distance and handled by tractor-trailer combinations, or by smaller trucks in the case of smaller businesses. Large tractor-trailer combinations and larger single-unit trucks have very different acceleration and deceleration characteristics from the automobile and mixing high volumes of truck traffic with automobiles creates an unsafe environment and reduces efficiency for the automobile and truck. This is particularly true as congestion levels increase.

Not all metropolitan urban areas have seaports, river connections or major rail facilities. However, many are home to large warehousing activities and might be considered land ports. At such warehousing facilities large loads are broken down for distribution and combined for long haul trips. Since loading, unloading and reloading can have significant impact on the efficiency of the freight transportation system, pallet loads and new containerization techniques allow for the more efficient transfer of goods. Containerization strategies can also improve security by reducing the number of times a container must be opened and the manner in which a container is tracked. Large retail operations are using RFID technology to track pallets of goods and extending inventory tracking concepts to the highway.

Urban freight environments offer an excellent opportunity to establish a use and price relationship: one that could be economically beneficial to the public and the shipper. While separate truck only facilities may not always be possible, truck only lanes may be designated during specific periods of the day. Over time, the fee paid by shippers would generate the funds necessary to construct permanent "truck only" lanes on public right of way.

Any of these concepts for moving urban freight must be analyzed on a project basis to determine the economic viability, the probable effect on urban traffic patterns and the proper contribution of the public and private sectors.

A prescription for Rural Freight Movement

The movement of freight in rural areas has similar characteristics to that of urban freight, however, for long distances rail is much more competitive, especially for bulk commodities such as coal, timber, etc. Airfreight is also more competitive for long distances but predominantly for high-value commodities. However, the truck is still the primary means of freight hauling in the U.S.

Rail competitiveness in the long-haul market could be increased but to do so would require improvements in the predictable arrival times. In a just-in-time market environment predictability is paramount and time lost in transit affects the ultimate value of goods. While rail vehicle speed does not differ from the tractor-trailer by a great deal, total trip time can be markedly different. Time is lost in rail yard operations as trains are disassembled and reassembled at major rail centers and this reduces the competitive advantage of the raw locomotive efficiency of rail. There are opportunities to apply similar technology to that employed used to track freight on the highway. Freight tracking through the use of RFID and GPS systems could be used to unitize railroad cars into trains at rail yards and perhaps reduce the time necessary to assemble trains for long-haul routes, thereby becoming more competitive with rubber-tire freight hauling. Further, by incorporating rail freight operations into freight intermodal centers, transfer between the modes of rail and highway could be more efficiently accomplished. Containerized freight which is identified by RFID tags that contain information about origin, destination, type of freight and delivery time requirements could be used to improve efficiency at intermodal transfer centers and perhaps help in the assembly of freight units for long distances. The use of better information on each container or unit of freight could be used to determine the most efficient mode for transfer to meet the requirements for delivery. While much cooperation between freight operators and the rail companies would be necessary, the technology nevertheless exists to support such an approach.

Pallet information could be electronically linked to the trailer or rail car on which it is traveling. The interfaces between systems would require common freight protocols and record formats that would accept the data. Ultimately, containerized freight might transit over several modes to the final destination. The design and regulation of such a system would require a governmental involvement to set standards and encourage cooperation in freight movement. Potentially rail cars and containers could be tracked electronically either with RFID or GPS and pallet information could be consolidated into the rail car information. Information about origin, destination and cargo could be used for routing freight and managing freight transfer at intermodal and rail centers. The result would be efficient, electronically operated rail yards. Rail yards could be the genesis of freight intermodal centers that would likely be located on the periphery of major urban areas. Cooperation between rail and highway movement and between companies at intermodal centers would improve freight efficiency and security.

Currently the tractor-trailer combination transports the majority of the volume and certainly the value of goods, even in long-haul situations. The exception is the movement of bulk commodities. Increasingly, the rural sections of the interstate highway system are congested as shown in current USDOT freight maps and projections for 2020 predict significant growth. This presents a similar issue to that just described in urban areas. The interstate system is the freight highway of the U.S. The concentration of freight travel on the interstate highway system has been stimulated by increased trade resulting from the North American Free Trade Agreement and travel between urban areas to meet the standards of just-in-time inventory control. A possible solution is to establish dedicated lanes for freight travel through urban areas. While the costs to construct "truck only" lanes over long distances are large, such proposals are being considered. For example, Texas is considering dedicated lanes between major seaport locations and borders with Mexico and has defined a 4,000 mile system of transportation corridor that would include "truck only" lanes constructed by the private sector.

In the long run it is not sustainable to support the growth of rural truck freight and automotive passenger travel growth on the same transportation infrastructure. Data indicates that by 2020, 60 per cent of the urban interstate highways and 35 per cent of the rural interstate highways will carry 10,000 or more trucks per day.[108] Such large volumes of truck traffic will be added to the growth of passenger automobile traffic, hastening congestion.

Dedicated truck lanes also offer the opportunity to apply technology that would allow for electronically linked vehicles to travel more efficiently and safely. Adaptive cruise control technology exists today that links several vehicles electronically into a train of vehicles. The result is greater fuel efficiency and a safer environment for heavy vehicles. Such systems use sensors to automatically maintain a safe distance from the vehicle ahead, adapting to speed changes and braking.

The growth projected for freight movement would suggest that any techniques that might separate trucks from passenger vehicles would result in an improvement in safety and travel time for both. Moving long-distance freight from the highway to the railway would also be advantageous, but to do so will require that railways find ways to compete on meeting delivery times in a predictable manner.

A Prescription for Rural Passenger Travel

Rural travel volume has accelerated for passenger vehicles just as it has for freight. Because air travel has been altered with the horrendous events of 9/11 and the resultant changes in airport security, there has been an increase of rural travel by automobile. More people are choosing to drive because of the time required to pass through security and the general concern about the safety of air travel. Some travelers believe that itineraries of less than 500 miles are just as easily accomplished by automobile as by air. Whether proven or not, the perception is causing a shift to more rural passenger travel. NASA has determined in its research on personal air vehicles that for travel distances of 100 to 500 miles consumers will use the automobile 20 times more often than aircraft.[109] This shift may not in itself represent a large economic impact from the perspective of time utility but there are certainly economic impacts being felt in the airline industry.

Rural rail passenger service has been subsidized through the operations of Amtrak with limited success. A mode that once was hailed as the economic engine of the U.S. and tied the eastern and western interests of the United States together, is now a subsidized operation. New ways must be found to stimulate Amtrak to compete in the rural passenger traffic market. In areas of the country with concentrations of population, air traffic congestion is becoming an increasing concern. As the demand for rural passenger travel increases, high-speed rail may become a major agenda. As with any major public works project there is always concern for seizing the initiative and investing in the future. The transcontinental railroad is an example of just such a situation. There are many commonalities between the two initiatives and high speed rail for rural passenger service may have similar long term economic impacts on the nation.

Rural passenger travel modes for the 100-to-500 mile range must be safe and economically competitive with automobile or airline alternatives and will likely not be so except in very concentrated corridors of population. It is also likely that public funding will be required to begin such projects though stimulated economic growth may provide the incentive for the private sector to consider investing. The European Union has adopted high-speed rail as an important part of the transportation strategy and is updating its high-speed rail systems, expanding the network throughout the European Union. While the United States has miles of rail network, it is almost exclusively owned by private interests and the operating arm of rural passenger service is a quasi-public agency. Europe is essentially the opposite; public-owned railways and the rolling stock operated by the private sector. For many reasons it is difficult to compare the Europe and the U.S. on rural rail passenger service, there may be some knowledge to gain by reviewing their strategy.

To begin connecting major population centers with high-speed rail will require an enormous investment, but it may be an investment that must be undertaken to sustain long-term economic growth, maintain the safety of airline travel and ensure a high quality of life. The core of America's economic power is currently 80 percent services based. If growth in the service sector is expected, passenger travel between major metropolitan areas will likely expand and will require a high-volume, high-speed transportation system.

Prescription Summary

Revitalizing the nation's transportation system will require bold action rather than incremental steps. Major changes will be required in the level of transportation funding, the source of funds, the degree of participation of the private sector, how public organizations are structured and the focus of U.S. transportation policy. The connection of major metropolitan areas of the country with high-speed, high-volume freight and passenger facilities must remain a focus and continued dependence on the existing interstate highway system may through expansion and pricing be adequate for some time to come but it is not the most efficient method of movement. Further, the transit of freight and passengers in the metropolitan areas must be addressed and with some sense of urgency. Congestion levels are reaching the point that delay will grow at a much quicker rate.

The last century saw the dramatic development of the finest transportation system in the world and it has supported the huge economic growth that has resulted in the largest economy in the world. Our standard of living and quality of life are intimately related to the adequacy of that transportation system.

Research has clearly established the relationship between the economy and the arterial highway system and the investment in the arterial system has begun to lag behind. The results of underinvestment are beginning to be seen in America's urban and rural areas, and will amplify in the short term, as the impacts grow in a non-linear manner.

Although general prescriptions have been offered herein, they are presented to generate discussion more than present a comprehensive solution. The issues of transportation policy are extremely complex and the formulation of transportation policy is a blend of data analysis, public choice and politics. Discussion, however, can not be the only result. Action is called for. The spirit and daring demonstrated by past leaders must be matched by the leaders of today.

Texas is indicative of the kind of "can do" attitude that must begin to prevail in other parts of the country, and particularly at the federal level. The passage of HB3588 and the subsequent signature by Governor Rick Perry on June 19, 2003 establishes a goal of constructing a Trans Texas Corridor, sanctions the establishment of regional mobility authorities in urban areas, and provides for unique and innovative financial strategies and assistance from the state. While it must be remembered that one size does not fit all, much can be learned from this initiative. In growth states, like Texas, bold action must be taken to improve transportation. Even though funds may not be immediately available to construct all intercity and intra-city facilities, a statement of the vision is essential. It is also clear that transportation is, of necessity, a multimodal endeavor, especially within urban areas, and that modal strategies are inherently linked for passenger service as well as freight movement.

6

"It is no use saying, 'We are doing our best'. You have got to succeed in doing what is necessary."

—*Winston Churchill*

THE POLITICAL WILL TO LEAD

Political will is about leadership. It includes the willingness to listen, formulate a direction and act decisively. Political will and leadership should not consist of playing to the press and special interest groups and then attempting to provide for those interests without defining resources. Such actions are however, the most likely way to get re-elected. Political leadership becomes moot if one is not reelected. It is this political catch 22 that makes political will a scarce commodity. The choice of leadership and resignation in politics is also what separates the career politician from the one that serves the public. The career politician is always planning how to achieve the next position, one can only hope that it is not at the expense of fulfilling the obligations of the current position.

To affect this cycle the public must become informed. It is incongruent that a public that wants sound government resigns itself to living with the results of government until it is directly affected in some way. This reality leaves the responsibility to inform with the media and the implementing agency. Public policy issues are inherently complex, multi-faceted, inter-related and numerous. In such an environment it is extremely difficult to be an informed citizen. The press is central to communicating the public policy debate to citizens and usually is the primary mechanism through which many of the public gain an understanding of the issues. Public understanding of policy issues should be the first step in affecting policymaking by government, not the last. And yet with such an enormous responsibility for the proper workings of government, the media have to balance between profitability and community leadership. Many factors in our political system contribute to this dilemma.

The media, campaign finance and the timing of the election cycle add to the issue. It is particularly pertinent in transportation because of the unique organizations which control the capital programs, the relationship of politics to transportation constituencies and the public perception and knowledge of the transportation process.

Large expenditures are necessary to accomplish the development of public works projects and contracts numbering in the millions and occasionally billions of dollars are let. Though construction is typically awarded based on low bid, many other activities are not. Design services are typically procured through uniform professional services contracts but many opportunities exist for selecting service providers on subjective criteria. The role of appointed officials, contractors and politicians frequently converge around transportation programs.

The Role of the Media

A media outlet that accepts the challenge of service to the community must report news that is sometimes not clamorous or even interesting. Contrary to the responsibility the press has for clarifying policy debates, a case can be made that the media furthers political confusion out of a desire to expand news value and thereby create profit.

In the first three quarters of the last century, the editors and publishers were the owners of the newspapers and radio stations and were likely local community leaders themselves. This is no longer the case. The conglomerate media outlets of today own multiple newspapers, radio stations or television stations and an argument can be made that the agenda has changed from one of local community activism and leadership to profitability. Media ratings and publication awards are precursors to advertisement revenues, stockholder equity and dividends. In such an environment, the political leader must attempt to inform and influence constituencies and the public at large.

A century ago it was common to have a local newspaper owned and operated by local members of the community. The publisher, owner, editor and, on occasion, the reporter were the same person. As metropolitan areas began to grow, the newspapers grew with them: but the newspapers remained locally owned, except in larger markets. The advent of radio and television as alternate news sources and the trend towards deregulation has resulted in the news media becoming increasingly owned by corporate interests. Though publishers are appointed with the intention of creating a local community presence, the corporate and community interests have begun to diverge.

The Telecommunications Act of 1996 and ensuing Federal Communications Commission rulemaking has further relaxed ownership restrictions. The merger and consolidation actions that occurred over the last 30 years have led to headquarters being located in major cities and removed from the local concerns of others. As with any other business, these conglomerates are interested in subscriptions and ultimately profitability. Newspapers also tend to compare their awards for reporting with others and the awards give a sense of value to the community and therefore the likelihood that subscriptions will increase. It is a beauty contest judged by the contestants. It is also common to find corporate news organizations with interests in television and radio.

Electronic media have gone through similar corporate consolidations as print and increasingly they are in the same corporation. The electronic media tend to use independent rating services to statistically report how many households are watching a given news show or production series. The dilemma comes in determining which story makes the 6 pm news, a public information story of importance to the community or the story that will give the reporter/TV star more attention and yield higher ratings. As these decisions are made, the service characteristics of the media outlet is decided. Profitability has led local media outlets to put forward the stories of most controversy and in depth coverage of complex issues have little opportunity in the world of the sound bite. The result is poor quality public information, further confusion of the public agenda and a misunderstanding of public decision making. Nevertheless, the news media are instrumental in establishing public opinion.

The press can inform through the direct provision of information from research or other credible sources or through a statement of opinion formulated by the leadership of the media company. Both are important methods for assisting the public to come to an informed decision whether on an important community issue or at the ballot box. Radio, television and print vary in their influence and the sectors of the public most likely to be affected and the degree of public information content. While radio and television are popular and offer the most content for the least amount of time invested, print has more permanency and provides more direct editorial comment.

Communications professionals understand the difference in standards between news reporting and editorial opinion, however the public at large does not. Reporters are admonished to provide a balanced, complete and verified report of news, while opinion writers are expected to gather information from various sources and form opinion. Though much research is conducted in the formation of opinions, the results are in the end subjective. Columnists are even more at liberty to express opinion free of editorial boards or other guidance. The public is not adept at differentiating between these sources of information and the differences in the research supporting the process. Though reporters are bound by standards of reporting based on verification of sources, the manner in which a topic is presented and the choice of words can affect the conclusions of the reader dramatically. In all cases the motivation of profitability is an underlying factor.

No where in the media is issue of competitiveness and profitability more prevalent than in television. It is remarkable to see the differences in news reporting during "sweeps" week. During the period surveys are conducted of viewers to determine ratings for the various local stations in terms of the market they penetrate. The market share reports directly affect the rates that the various stations can charge for advertising and therefore the profitability of the station. News stories that have the most attention getting potential are always released during this period. Stations have been known to hold reports for the sweeps week in order to affect the outcome of the ratings. In this process of media communications the public official must function.

The elected official's role in public policy formulation is at the core of a democratic representative government. Obviously, elected officials are influenced by media reports about their positions on policy, especially in an election year and while researched information may be available, many depend upon popular materials published by the news media. They are quite reluctant to take a position that might vary with popular opinion as expressed by the media.

There are frequent reports of the need for transportation facilities but rarely does the media publish information on the extent of the need for funds. Articles abound on issues like suburbanization and the inherent inefficiency of providing services to remote urban centers spawned by suburbanization, but little is communicated about how or why the U.S. has suburbanized. Opinions are frequently given on modal choice and the need to develop transit. There is however little presented about why people make the choices that they do and in the end rather than serving to create understanding of the issues, the media feeds controversy. There is little discussion on how to bring about a balanced, multimodal transportation program that is sustainable and fundable. Consequently, the funding needed to carry out transportation programs receive little mention or support.

The Appointment Process

Transportation agency leadership is a combination of executive and agency board appointments. The former is sometimes selected based on political activism but more often they are based on transportation expertise. Boards and commissions however, are typically selected because of their political activity. The role of the board is usually as the appointed representatives of the people and the statutory authority is usually vested in the board, while the staff leadership is more technical and operational in nature. The political appointment process for boards varies but appointees are generally able to attract election campaign funding and are active campaigning. The interests of potential appointees is considered and availability of appointed positions of course will affect the appointment process. Many political appointees, and elected officials therefore are ill equipped to provide specific direction to complex policy areas such as transportation. Although appointed for the express purpose of representing the public, their effectiveness depends on the expertise of professionals in the field of concern. For this reason, policy board members and professional staffs must build a rapport of trust and directness. A balance between expertise and political input must be achieved.

The Election Timeline

The focus of political decision-making is election. Because of the short cycle of the election process and the long period of time required to fund and construct a transportation project, a unique political interaction with transportation policy occurs. The typical election cycle is four years for most federal, state and local offices, with the exception of the United States Senate, which is six years. The typical cycle to develop a major transportation project from concept to and through construction is usually ten or more years and that assumes that funds are available at each milestone. Many projects are in process for 12 to 15 years and in some cases are abandoned for lack of funding. It is beyond the horizon of political planning to consider long-term economic trends, which extend twenty, thirty or more years.

This difference in election cycle and transportation development cycle have allowed politicians to support "silver bullet" solutions such as technology, alternate modes, or even single projects as the solution to congestion. By the time the community realizes that at best, the solution is partial, the politician has moved on. The lasting memory of political action is the candidate's ability to procure funds for key projects. The election cycle contrasted to the time required to develop a transportation project is a synchronization that will not likely occur but it should be kept in mind.

Political Aspects of Transportation Funding

Toll roads are the only mechanism available to establish a reasonable pricing to use relationship. For all of the reasons presented, there is a general malaise about providing adequate funding and generally the public has reached a position that they are unwilling to pay for public works infrastructure. Strangely, this is in contrast to other basic public infrastructure such as water and electricity, which are commonly capitalized through a usage fee. Further, electricity is commonly provided through private regulated utility companies and many water systems are privatized.

At the heart of public works policy is finance, and it is the politicians who appropriate the funds for transportation or those who control the executive branch where transportation funds are administered that can influence funding decisions. In this environment there are several givens. First, the politician "wants to have his cake and eat it too." In essence the politician wants it to appear that transportation can be provided without the necessary taxation. It has become very difficult to remain an elected official if even a hint of possibility exists for transportation taxation. Any other possibility that might result in improvements to transportation will receive the attention of the politician first.

This aligns perfectly with the expectations of the public who have come to expect very high levels of transportation at a perceived price of zero and this has given rise to the "silver bullet." A "silver bullet" is something that appears to resolve a very complex and fundamental problem with a new and certain solution. The application of technology is frequently perceived to be a solution and is too often a "sliver bullet." "Silver bullets" also come in the form of new transportation programs or even single projects. Occasionally, the introduction of a new program will have the support of a powerful special interest group or constituency whose support is needed for re-election. Any of these agenda redirects the focus from the core issue of sufficient transportation funding and taxation. "Silver bullet" solutions frequently turn out to be mirages, but by then the political cycle has been completed and someone new is faced with resolving the issues in transportation. At this point they have likely become more pronounced.

Public Perception

It is a common belief of the general public that many of the resources available for public programs are wasted and transportation is no different. This perception is occasionally fed by events but in the main it is mistaken. The largest expenditure in transportation is for capital construction or major maintenance. These activities are contracted to the private sector and awarded to the lowest bidder. A properly administered low bid process ensures optimum efficiency through the marketplace.

Much of the design of major projects is also contracted to the private sector through a competitive negotiation for professional services. The highest quality proposal is selected, the hours required to perform the work are negotiated and the price is determined through a calculation of actual salary and overhead. Profits in the engineering design business are typically in the 10 per cent range.

Perceptions persist about wasted resources in transportation for several reasons. First, the process of funding is overly complex and confusing. The federal funding process is the result of almost 100 years of categorical funding that attempts to provide national uniformity and set transportation policy. This is overlaid with state categorical funding, which further complicates and is intended to affect local decisions. In addition, each of these levels of government has its own sources of transportation funding and it is not clear to the public which funds have been used on a given project or why. The result is that the public does not see a connection between resources and projects. The concept of "getting what you pay for" is lost and leads the public to assume that the resources are wasted.

The second reason the public believes that sufficient resources exist for transportation is the manner in which the media communicates. A favorite topic of the media is government waste. While waste undoubtedly exists, it is reported on frequently and leaves the impression that it is a common phenomenon throughout government. Rarely does a report by the media identify the connection between paying for transportation and using it and the need for additional transportation facilities.

It is convenient to conclude that money has been wasted because it excludes debate for more revenue and higher taxes. This is further amplified when politicians state, "All that is needed is for the government to become more efficient," or when no-tax coalitions make similar comments opposing any new taxation. Those who must pay any increases in taxation have a propensity to believe such reports and comments.

The communications between the public and those elected to represent them can reinforce one another. Political candidates commonly advocate "no new taxes"; a message the public wants to hear. The voter uses the complexity of the issue to conclude that funding is sufficient and both conclude that all that is needed is to eliminate the waste. The media have an obligation to bring the facts to the debate.

Campaign Finance

Fundamental to the ability to be elected is sufficient campaign funding to operate in an era of mass communications. Without funds to "get the word out" it is next to impossible to compete in the electoral process. Transportation is a policy area that requires large amounts of public funds and attracts a large vendor community. Consequently, the many special interests groups involved in transportation are a major source of campaign funding. Engineers, contractors, bond underwriters, lawyers and developers are typically active in the process of soliciting for campaign funds. While the public at large can be involved in gathering campaign funds, the conglomeration of small donations leaves the individual with much less impact on the political agenda of the politician. While it is more efficient to attract a few large contributions rather than a large number of small contributions, the process can erode the trust of the public and generate concerns about supporting transportation programs.

Political action committees of various associated businesses, special interest organizations, citizens against taxes and others are all in the process of gathering funds to elect an official that will do their bidding. Few if any of these consider a transportation policy beyond what it may do for their interest. Their ability to deliver funds however, causes politicians to respond in ways not necessarily in the interests of the public at large. Once the politician is elected, those who contributed are more likely to receive some benefit and the cycle repeats. Perhaps one of the most pressing issues in America is campaign finance reform.

Earmarking Funds

Another component of transportation funding that negatively affects the public confidence is the practice of earmarking transportation expenditures, and a version of this political process can occur at any level of government. Earmarking is the process of setting out a project above all others by appropriating funds directly to a project rather than attempting to fund the project through the allocation process. Earmarking precludes the necessity to compete with other projects on the basis of need. These earmarks are sometimes termed "pork" because of the political nature of the decision making process. Of course, each constituencies believes that earmarking is a reasonable process if it is their project that gets approved, but an extremely poor process when some one else's project is earmarked, especially if it uses funds that would have otherwise been available for their project.

In today's transportation policy environment one must work the process or be left behind in the earmarking game. The number of projects earmarked in the federal reauthorization process have grown tremendously from the passage of ISTEA in 1991. Lobbyists are hired by public agencies to assist in this process and many times they are ex-politicians or high level officials in the executive branch who have contacts and access to those currently in government. The process of earmarking does not however instill confidence in the public eye and furthers the perception that transportation programs are wasteful. If money can be set aside through earmarking and the core transportation agenda remains seemingly unaffected, the conclusion is that a surplus of funds exist dedicated to transportation.

Earmarking plays a large role in the election process. If a senator or representative at the federal or state level can take credit for bringing a major transportation project to a community, the chances of re-election are greatly improved. The earmarking of transportation funds has become a self perpetuating process.

On the other extreme from political earmarking is categorical funding. Categorical funding attempts to control transportation policy through allocation to specific policy agendas and can also contribute to the confusion felt by the public. Further, dividing the funding into so many discrete categories at each level of government makes it difficult to accumulate sufficient funding on a project to actually construct it. To move a project schedule forward, earmarking becomes even more attractive and agencies have become more dependent upon lobbyists and their contacts with the politicians. The processes of earmarking and categorical fund allocations serve to further the disconnection between the payment of a tax for transportation and the resultant project.

The Political Decision Making Process

The political decision making process varies significantly between the various levels of government. Federal, state and local government have similar agenda in transportation but emphasize policy areas uniquely.

The federal level of government has historically set transportation policy and ensured compliance through the threat of withdrawal of funding from states which do not comply. While many of these policy agenda are in the interests of the safety of the traveling public, the threat of withholding federal funds can ultimately lead to poor pubic policy. Strong federal regulation has brought about uniformity in action by the states and has ensured that standards of construction, design and right of way acquisition are consistent. The desire to control policy and yet avoid taxation can lead to poor public policy. For example, the federal government and the Congress has concluded that the construction of the interstate system of highways has been completed and that funds allocated for construction of new interstate highway capacity should be phased out. Therefore, if any new construction of interstate capacity is to occur, it must come from funds allocated in other categories or from state funds generated by state gasoline tax. Similarly, federal policy limits the degree to which federal funds can be used for maintenance or operations of facilities. Consequently, the system that has the most impact on economic vitality and the system demonstrating some of the fastest growing needs is losing traditional sources of funding. Because the interstate was funded 90% federal and 10% state, it is very difficult for state and local governments to raise sufficient capital to expand or maintain the system. The devolution of taxation from the federal to the state and local levels may in the end, result in devolution to direct user pricing and concessions.

Similar issues arise on other major transportation programs besides highway construction and maintenance and states have devolved responsibility to the local level. States have accepted the need to fund maintenance of roadways but have been reluctant to become involved in the labor component of operating for bus and rail systems and increasingly the labor required to operate traffic control centers for ITS projects. Because of these events local governments have carried the burden through local taxation. These developments do not however, assist in the strategic development of transportation systems based on need and public preference but rather based on the vagaries of politics and incremental funding.

The return of federal gasoline tax collected in a state is yet another process which has little to do with funding transportation and more to do with politics. States are adamant about receiving their full share of the federal gasoline tax collected in their respective states and yet are in a similar role in allocating funds to specific regions within the state. Larger municipal areas that generate a greater proportion of transportation taxes at the state level similarly want those taxes returned to their geographical area. Precisely the same argument that the states have with the federal government. However, in this case state agencies argue vehemently for a redistribution of allocations. This continuous discussion of allocation and fairness in the transportation process detracts from the larger question of adequate funding.

With the passage of the ISTEA bill in 1991, greater involvement in project priority was defined for the metropolitan planning organizations. Taken in the context of the allocation issues just discussed, this provision only succeeds in further confusing the issue of adequate transportation funding. Without sufficient funding available to satisfy the growing transportation needs, some state departments of transportation have abdicated their responsibility for prioritizing projects to the MPOs and local politics.

There is also the practice of expanding the use of transportation funds that were generated by the gasoline tax. The gasoline tax was originally put in place to fund roads and as such the perception of the public is that those funds are dedicated to that purpose. As the nation urbanized in the last half of the century and many of the privately operated transit companies began to fail, the function became a government activity. Overtime greater portions of the gasoline tax were used to fund public transit in various forms. The capital required for buses, bus facilities, light rail and commuter rail have all been funded from this source. Further, these funds are not subject to the state allocation rules as categorical funds, a trait shared with earmarked funds. While an appropriate and valid use of transportation funding, the connection to the gasoline tax was confusing. Was gasoline tax to be used for highways or for transportation in general? If it is for transportation in general then why isn't gasoline tax used to fund the construction of freight intermodal centers or airport construction? The gasoline tax as a source of funding is not only inadequate for the amount of funds needed but it is philosophically inadequate to the task of funding the many transportation agenda of today.

It is an accepted fact that to get support for tax increases there must be a connection between the payment of the tax and the benefit expected. Site specific surveys have shown repeatedly that the public is willing to accept new taxation if it believes that there is accountability for results. The public's perception of the transportation process, however, is that it lacks credibility. Public agencies that deliver a product for a fee, such as water, sewer, waste disposal, etc., would not consider using part of the water charge for another service. Further, they perceive citizens as customers. Services must have a direct connection between price and benefit for the provider as well as the customer.

The Role of the Politician

To change the process of transportation funding will require political leadership. In Plato's The Republic, "politician" was not a vocation but rather a service that was provided by those best able to serve. It was an ideal that was required for healthy governance. Today, politician is a vocation, just as a teacher, a policeman or an accountant is. We often hear of those who have served well at one level expecting to move to the next, and we expect the same. Political leadership should not consist of pleasing the majority; it should be about accomplishing something of value for the republic. Such a view is considered naïve, and perhaps ideals have become synonymous with naiveté. For the good of the republic let us hope that is not the case.

APPENDIX

Table 11: Hypothetical Roadway—10 Years Average Growth

Hour	Volume	34% 10 yr @ 3% Vol>Cap.	Increase Cum.	Delay (Min.)
12-1AM	202	-2048		
1-	202	-2048		
2-	202	-2048		
3-	202	-2048		
4-	202	-2048		
5-	202	-2048		
6-	806	-1444		
7-	1210	-1040		
8-	2016	-234		
9-	2621	371	371	10
10-	2822	572	943	25
11-	2218	-32	911	24
Noon-1	2419	169	1080	29
1-	2218	-32	1048	28
2-	2016	-234	814	22
3-	2419	169	983	26
4-	2621	371	1354	36
5-	2218	-32	1321	35
6-	1210	-1040	281	7
7-	806	-1444		
8-	403	-1847		
9-	403	-1847		
10-	403	-1847		
11-Mid.	403	-1847		
	30442 Volume	-23558 Vol>Cap.		243 (Min.)

155

Table 12: Hypothetical Roadway—15 Years Average Growth

Hour	Volume	Increase 56% 15 yr @ 3% Vol>Cap.	Cum.	Delay (Min.)
12-1AM	234	-2016		
1-	234	-2016		
2-	234	-2016		
3-	234	-2016		
4-	234	-2016		
5-	234	-2016		
6-	936	-1314		
7-	1404	-846		
8-	2340	90	90	2
9-	3042	792	882	24
10-	3276	1026	1908	51
11-	2574	324	2232	60
Noon-1	2808	558	2790	74
1-	2574	324	3114	83
2-	2340	90	3204	85
3-	2808	558	3762	100
4-	3042	792	4554	121
5-	2574	324	4878	130
6-	1404	-846	4032	108
7-	936	-1314	2718	72
8-	468	-1782	936	25
9-	468	-1782		
10-	468	-1782		
11-Mid.	468	-1782		
	35334 Volume	-18666 Vol>Cap.		936 (Min.)

Table 13: Hypothetical Roadway—20 Years Average Growth

Hour	Volume	81% 20 yr @ 3% Vol>Cap.	Increase Cum.	Delay (Min.)
12-1AM	314	-1936	4487	120
1-	314	-1936	2551	68
2-	314	-1936	616	16
3-	314	-1936		
4-	314	-1936		
5-	314	-1936		
6-	1257	-993		
7-	1885	-365		
8-	3142	892	892	24
9-	4085	1835	2728	73
10-	4399	2149	4877	130
11-	3457	1207	6084	162
Noon-1	3771	1521	7605	203
1-	3457	1207	8811	235
2-	3142	892	9704	259
3-	3771	1521	11225	299
4-	4085	1835	13060	348
5-	3457	1207	14267	380
6-	1885	-365	13902	371
7-	1257	-993	12909	344
8-	628	-1622	11287	301
9-	628	-1622	9666	258
10-	628	-1622	8044	215
11-Mid.	628	-1622	6423	171
	47451 Volume	-6549 Vol>Cap.		3977 (Min.)

Endnotes

1. The World Fact book, United States Central Intelligence Agency, 2002, http://www.odci.gov/cia/publications/factbook/geos/ve.html#Econ.

2. Federal Highway Administration and Bureau of Transportation Statistics, Washington, DC: United States Department of Transportation, 2003.

3. Federal Highway Administration, *Highway Statistics*, Washington, DC: U.S Department of Transportation; and International Road Federation, *World Road Statistics 2002*, Washington, DC: International Road Federation, 2002.

4. Transportation Quarterly, Summer 2003, Vol. 57, No. 3, March 20, 2003, John Pucher and John L. Renne.

5. Wright, James; Fixin to Get, One Fan's Love Affair with NASCAR's Winston Cup, Duke University Press, Durham North Carolina, page 33, 2002.

6. Economic Implications of Congestion; Glen Weisbrod, Donald Vary, and George Treyz; National Cooperative Highway Research Program, Report Number 463, Page 42, National Academy Press, Washington D.C., 2001.

7. Scale, Congestion and Growth, Theo Eicher and Steven Turnovsky, University of Washington, May 1998, Page 26.

8. Aschauer, D. A. (1989b) Does Public Capital Crowd out Private Capital?" *Journal of Monetary Economics* 24: 171-188, and Aschauer, D. A. (1989a) Is Public Expenditure Productive? *Journal of Monetary Economics* 23: 177-200.

9. National Cooperative Highway Research Program, Project 2-17(3), FY 1993, Macroeconomic Analysis of the Linkages Between Transportation Investments and Economic Performance, Michael Bell and Therese McGuire, October 1994.

10. Coyle, John; Bardi, Edward; Novack Robert; Transportation—Fourth Edition; West Publishing Company; 1994, page 5.

11. American Society of Civil Engineers, Report Card for America's Infrastructure, 1998, http://www.pubs.asce.org/news/sep5.html.

12. How Traffic Congestion is Putting the Brakes on Economic Growth, The Road Information Program, Washington D.C., May 2001.

13. Caldwell, Harry. "I-Freight, The Role of the Interstate Highway System in Freight Transportation." Interstate Vision Initiative, USDOT, Office of Freight Management and Operations.

14. Ibid.

15. Florida Chamber Foundation, Transportation Cornerstone: Moving Florida's Economy into the 21st Century, January 1999, page 23

16. Bureau of Transportation Statistics, USDOT, Freight Shipments in America 2004, http://www.bts.gov/publications/freight_shipments_in_america/excel/table_01.xls.

17. Environmental Advantages of Inland Barge Transportation, United States Department of Transportation, Maritime Administration, August 1994.

18. Cox, Wendell and Love, Jean. "40 Years of the US Interstate Highway System: An Analysis, The Best Investment A Nation Ever Made." (June, 1996), http://www.publicpurpose.com/freeway1.htm.

19. USDOT, Federal Highway Administration, Turner Fairbank Highway Research Center, summer 1996, Volume 60, No. 1, Washington D.C.

20. Garver, Lori. "Next-Generation Space Transportation, Six (hopefully) Interesting Thoughts in Sixty Seconds." DFI International, Washington D.C. (May 2001).

21. "Canada-United States Trade Relationship," United States Commercial Service, United States Department of Commerce, 2001. http://www.buyusa.gov/canada/en/page33.html.

22. Moore, Thomas, "Trucking Deregulation," The library of Economics and Liberty, The Concise Encyclopedia of Economics, 1993, http://www.econlib.org/library/Enc/TruckingDeregulation.html.

23. Ibid.

24. The World Fact book, United States Central Intelligence Agency, 2002., http://www.odci.gov/cia/publications/factbook/geos/ve.html#Econ.

25. Ibid.

26. Viae, The Roads of Rome." KET Distance Learning can be found at: www.dl.ket.org/latin3/mores/techno/roads.

27. Hansen, Roger. "Water and Wastewater Systems in Imperial Rome," http://www.waterhistory.org/histories/rome.

28. Costs, Benefits and Consequences—An Alternative Environmental Strategy, Program Manager, Michael E. Heberling, May-June 1995, Page 36, http://www.dau.mil/pubs/pm/pmpdf95/heberlin.pdf.

29. Wikipedia, *The Free Encyclopedia,* Gardening, Wikimedia Foundation, St. Petersburg, Florida. http://en2.wikipedia.org/wiki/Gardens.

30. An Introduction to Transportation Engineering, William W. Hay, John Wiley & Sons, New York, 1961, Page 4.

31. Michigan's Internet Railroad History Museum, http://www.michiganrailroads.com and the National Railroad Museum, http://nationalrrmuseum.org.

32. Ambrose, Steven. "Nothing Like it in the World, The Men Who Built the Transcontinental Railroad," Simon and Schuster, New York, September 2000.

33. Daimler, Gottlieb and Benz, Karl, "Fascinating Facts About the Invention of the Modern Automobile," 1989, http://www.ideafinder.com/history/inventions/story054.htm.

34. Sources: USDOT, Bureau of Transportation Statistics, *National Transportation Statistics 2002* (Washington, DC: 2002), table 1-44.

35. 2001 air carriers—USDOT, Bureau of Transportation Statistics, *Air Carrier Traffic Statistics* (Washington, DC: Annual December issues).

36. Bureau of Transportation Statistics, USDOT, 1960-2000, http://www.bts.gov/publications/national_transportation_statistics/2002/html/table_01_11.html, and Public Broadcasting System, Global Connections, 1910, 1923 and 1929, http://www.pbs.org/wgbh/globalconnections/liberia/educators/uspolicy/lesson1.html

37. Federal Highway Administration and Bureau of Transportation Statistics, Washington, D.C.: United States Department of Transportation, 2002.

38. http://www.landandfreedom.org/ushistory/us13.htm.

39. Nativity of the Population and Place of Birth of the Native Population: 1850 to 1990, United States Bureau of the Census, March 9, 1999. http://www.census.gov/population/www/documentation/twps0029/tab01.html.

40. Budget of the United States Government, *Fiscal Year 2004,* Historical Tables, Table 1.1, http://w3.access.gpo.gov/usbudget/fy2004/hist.html.

41. Hardin, Garrett, The Tragedy of the Commons, Science, Vol 162, Issue 3859, 1243-1248, December 13, 1968.

42. "The Bottom Line", American Association of State Highway and Transportation Officials, Washington D.C., 2002.

43. Ibid.

44. National Transportation Statistics 2003, Bureau of Transportation Statistics, United States Department of Transportation, 1960-2000, Table 1-32, Page 53.

45. Transportation Cost and Benefit Analysis—Congestion Costs, Victoria Transport Policy Institute (www.vtpi.org).

46. 2002 Urban Mobility Study, Texas Transportation Institute, University of Texas, Austin, Texas, 2002. http://tti.tamu.edu/documents/mobility_report_2004.pdf.

47. ibid.

48. "Transportation Cornerstone Florida—Moving Florida's Economy into the 21st Century", Cambridge Systematics, January 1999, page 23, www.flchamber.com/home/transportation_cornerstone.asp.

49. "North American Commercial Vehicle Industry: 2002 The Year of the Roller Coaster", A.C.T. Research Company LLC, Columbus, IN, 2002, http://www.chicagofed.org/newsandevents/conferences/auto_outlook02/vieth.pdf.

50. ibid, 2002 Urban Mobility Study.

51. Sources: USDOT, Bureau of Transportation Statistics, *National Transportation Statistics 2002* (Washington, DC: 2002), Table 2-1, Pages 117-119.

52. ibid.

53. ibid, Table 2-2 and Table 2-3, Pages 120-125.

54. ibid.

55. http://www.asl-associates.com/vio1.htm.

56. http://www.asl-associates.com/Images/53nacty.pdf.

57. A.S.L. Associates, Helena, Montana, asl@attglobal.net.

58. 2002 Urban Mobility Study, Texas Transportation Institute, University of Texas, Austin, Texas, 2002.

59. The Bottom Line, American Association of State Highway and Transportation Officials, Washington D.C., 2002, Page 26.

60. 2002 Bottomline Report, American Association of State Highway and Transportation Officials, Washington D.C., 2002.

61. CIA World Factbook.

62. European Transport Policy For 2010: Time to Decide, European Commission White Paper, Directorate-General for Energy and Transport, September 2001.

63. European Transport Policy For 2010: Time to Decide, European Commission White Paper, Directorate-General for Energy and Transport, September 2001.

64. Investing in China Risky but Inviting, Glassman, James K., February 15,2004.

65. China's Tenth Five-Year Plan for National Economic and Social Development, www.chinacp.com/eng/cppolicystrategy/10th_5_ intro.htm.

66. http://www.globalsecurity.org/military/world/china/infras.htm, GlobalSecurity.org, 300 N. Washington St., Suite B-100, Alexandria, VA 22314.

67. The World Fact book, United States Central Intelligence Agency, 2004,http://www.odci.gov/cia/publications/factbook/geos/ ve.html#Econ

68. ibid.

69. World Reference Atlas, Dorling Kindersley Publishing, New York, New York, 1996, Page 169.

70. American Petroleum Institute, http://www.lmoga.com/taxrates. htm, 1/07/2003.

71. Motor Fuel Tax Rates for Selected Countries, USDOT, FHWA, May   2001,   http://www.fhwa.dot.gov/ohim/mmfr/feb01/ frgso5010201.htm.

72. Canadian Federation of Independent Business, news release February 13, 2003.

73. Bureau of Transportation Statistics, US Department of Transportation, www.bts.gov/laws_and_regulations/docs/isteal.htm.

74. Buchanan, James m., The Demand and Supply of Public Goods, Rand McNally & Company, Chicago, 1968.

75. Tracking the American Dream—Fifty years of Housing Changes, Statistical Brief, Bureau of Census, SB/94-8, April 1994.

76. Bureau of Transportation Statistics, USDOT, 1960-2000, http://www.bts.gov/publications/national_transportation_statistics/2002/html/table_01_11.html

77. Travel Trends in U.S. Cities: Explaining the 2000 Census Commuting Results, Peter Gordon, Bumsoo Lee, Harry W. Richardson, Lusk Center for Real Estate, University of Southern California, Los Angeles, CA, April, 2004, Table 2.1. Average commute length, time, and distance from NPTS/NHTS, 1983-2001

78. Alameda Corridor Transportation Authority, Draft Report, March 1995, http://www.scbbs.com/alameda/alameda.htm.

79. Alameda Corridor Freight Line, CA, USA, The Website for the Railway Industry, November 2003. http://www.railway-technology.com/projects/alameda.

80. Bureau of Transportation Statistics, USDOT, Washington, DC, 2003, Table 1-32. http://www.bts.gov/publications/national_transportation_statistics/2003/html/table_01_32.html.

81. 2002 Business Travel Survey, Business Travel Coalition, April 23, 2002, http://btcweb.biz/travelsurvey.htm.

82. Calculated from Table 1: Commercial Freight Activity by Mode 1993 and 2002, ($777 billion/2000*10 million tons)

83. Caldwell, Harry. "I-Freight, The Role of the Interstate Highway System in Freight Transportation," Interstate Vision Initiative, USDOT, Office of Freight Management and Operations.

84. "Regarding Ohio's Federal Transportation Funding Agenda", Testimony before the Transportation, Infrastructure and Nuclear Safety Subcommittee of the Senate Environment and Public Works Committee, Gordon Proctor, Director Ohio Department of Transportation, September 30, 2002.

85. Economic Implications of Congestion; Glen Weisbrod, Donald Vary, and George Treyz; National Cooperative Highway Research Program, Report Number 463, Page 42, National Academy Press, Washington D.C., 2001.

86. Economic Benefits of the Melbourne City Link, Allen Consulting, Melbourne 1994.

87. The Economic Effects of Federal Spending on Infrastructure and Other Investments, Congressional Budget Office, Nabeel Alsalam, Perry Beider, Kathy Gramp, and Philip Webre, June 1998.

88. Stuck in Traffic, May 2001, The Road Information Program, Washington D.C., Page 2.

89. Buchanan, James M., The Demand and Supply of Public Goods, Rand McNally & Company, Chicago, 1968.

90. London Congestion Pricing—Implications for Other Cities, Todd Litman, Victoria Transport Policy Institute, June 30, 2003, page 6, www.vtpi.org/london.pdf.

91. Rawls, John, "Theory of Justice", The Belknap Press of Harvard University Press, Cambridge, Massachusetts,1971.

92. http://www.tollroads.com/history.htm.

93. ibid.

94. ibid.

95. Facts and Myths About Tolls, A Compilation of Reference Materials, International Bridge, Tunnel, and Turnpike Association, Washington, D.C. page 19, May 2001.

96. This estimate is based on data from the state of Florida. In 2000 legislation removed appropriations to general fund agencies from the gasoline tax that represented the cost to collect. This was approximately 6% of the gasoline tax revenue in those years.

97. http://www.sfmuseum.org/hist/standoil.html.

98. National Transportation Statistics 2003, Bureau of Transportation Statistics, United States Department of Transportation, 1960-2000, Table 1-1, page 3 and Table 1-32, page 53.

99. Bureau of Transportation Statistics, USDOT, 1960-2000, http://www.bts.gov/publications/national_transportation_statistics/2002/html/table_01_11.html.

100. ibid.

101. USDOT, National Highway Traffic Safety Administration, *Automotive Fuel Economy Program: Annual Update Calendar Year 2001*, September 2001, table II-6, available at ww.nhtsa.dot.gov/cars/problems/studies, as of October 2002.

102. Planet Ark, "US 2001 Vehicle Mileage Falls to 20 Year Low—EPA", http://www.planetark.com/dailynewsstory.cfm/newsid/12678/story.htm.

103. National Transportation Statistics 2002, Bureau of Transportation Statistics, US Department of Transportation, Table 4-38: Estimated National Average Vehicle Emissions Rates by Vehicle Type and Fuel (Grams per mile), page 322.

104. US Environmental Protection Agency, Office of Mobile Sources, EPA 400-F-92-007 "Automobile Emissions: An Overview", August 1994. http://www.epa.gov/region5/air/mobile/auto_emis.htm

105. US Environmental Protection Agency, Office of Mobile Sources, EPA 400-F-92-005, "Automobiles and Carbon Monoxide", January 1993, page 2.

106. Florida Chamber Foundation, Transportation Cornerstone: Moving Florida's Economy into the 21st Century, January 1999, page 23.

107. http://www.scbbs.com/alameda/alameda.htm

108. Caldwell, Harry. "I-Freight, The Role of the Interstate Highway System in Freight Transportation," Interstate Vision Initiative, USDOT, Office of Freight Management and Operations.

109. NASA Explores Personal Air Vehicles That Can Dramatically Improve Mobility, NASA Aerospace Vehicle Systems Technology Office, Langley Research Center, Hampton, Virginia, Page 2, avst.larc.nasa.gov/downloads/PAVE%20NASA%20Facts%20new.pdf.

978-0-595-36643-9
0-595-36643-0

CPSIA information can be obtained at www.ICGtesting.com
Printed in the USA
LVOW12s0250220116

471822LV00001B/31/P